LAST ROMANTICS

Michael Lewis MacLennan

Last Romantics

Michael Lewis MacLennan

Playwrights Canada Press
Toronto • Canada

Last Romantics © Copyright 2003 Michael Lewis MacLennan
The moral rights of the author are asserted.

Playwrights Canada Press
54 Wolseley St., 2nd floor Toronto, Ontario CANADA M5T 1A5
416-703-0013   fax 416-703-0059
orders@playwrightscanada.com • www.playwrightscanada.com

Playwrights Canada Press acknowledges the support of
the taxpayers of Canada and the province of Ontario through
The Canada Council for the Arts and the Ontario Arts Council.

The Canada Council for the Arts
Le Conseil des Arts du Canada

ONTARIO ARTS COUNCIL
CONSEIL DES ARTS DE L'ONTARIO

Cover: Wood-engraving by Charles Ricketts: "Daphnis plucks from the top-
most bough... the reddening topmost apple." From the collection of Stephen
Calloway, reprinted with kind permission.
Production Editor: Jodi Armstrong

National Library of Canada Cataloguing in Publication

MacLennan, Michael Lewis, 1968-
      Last romantics / Michael Lewis MacLennan.

A play.
ISBN 0-88754-676-5

      I. Title.

PS8575.L45855L38 2003   C812'.54   C2003-903849-1

First edition: July 2003.
Printed and bound by AGMV Marquis at Quebec, Canada.

for Brian Pace and Brigitte Potter-Mäl

*artists who know love
and loss*

—•— Acknowledgements —•—

It's doubtful that I could have written *Last Romantics* without the research and writings of J.G.P. Delaney, Ricketts's biographer. His book *Charles Ricketts, A Biography* is unquestionably the authority on Ricketts and his circle. I thank Christopher Newton and the Shaw Festival for commissioning the play. Early drafts of the play were brilliantly dramaturged by Brian Quirt; I owe much to him. Special thanks also to Iris Turcott and Bill Glassco, who have helped at crucial stages.

Others have given advice, information and support over the past three years: Don Bachardy, Bruce Borysiuk, Martin Bragg, Miranda Burgess, Stephen Calloway, Mathias Chêne, Catriona Craig, Rod Christiansen, Luke Dixon, Jerry Doiron, Damon D'Oliveira, Warren Dunford, Brad Fraser, Michael Hoppe, Lise Ann Johnson, Michael Macaulay, Marti Maraden, Duncan McIntosh, Johanna Mercer, Michael Pantazzi and the National Gallery of Canada, Angela Rebeiro, Matt Rippy, Julie Salverson, Duncan Stewart, Leonie Sturge Moore, Claire Walker, and the British Library. Thanks also to the actors who participated in workshops, especially Liza Balkan, Ian Clark, Nora McLellan, Jim Mezon, Fiona Reid and Michael Schultz. And finally, my deepest thanks to Richard Rose who, with Necessary Angel and the National Arts Centre, said yes.

What is beauty? How do we know it when we see it? What's its point anyway? For some, the ideal of beauty was more than just an adornment of life – it was the essence of life, the very reason we build a civilisation. But in clinging to their convictions, many devotees of beauty had to make profound sacrifices.

In 1994 I came across a portrait of Charles Ricketts and Charles Shannon in England's National Portrait Gallery. Like most people, I'd never heard of these two artists, but there was something in their clear eyes, their open expressions and the brief accompanying biographies, which intrigued me. So I started foraging about libraries and soon had dived into these two men's remarkable fifty-year relationship. I was struck by their staggering triumphs and losses. I was also intrigued by how completely we could forget such brilliant and significant artists.

Ricketts and Shannon were arguably the most intelligent and passionate proponents of the æsthetic movement – an art movement that had its heyday in the last years of the 1800s. But in art, as in life, timing is everything. These two artists arrived late on the scene, and so lived in the face of a virulently modern world which saw them as old-fashioned. Their ideals, rich in imagination and mythologys, were being stripped down to fit new fashions. *Last Romantics* explores not only how and why we remember, but what, as individuals and as a culture, we forget. In telling the story of this remarkable relationship, I hope to explore the notion of failure, showing both the necessity and the folly of beauty in the modern world.

—M.L.M.

In London of the 1890s, the artists Charles Ricketts (1866-1931) and Charles Shannon (1863-1937) stood for certain æsthetic values. These were also shared by Oscar Wilde, who challenged Victorian moralism by insisting on "Art for Art's sake." He dazzled contemporaries with his wit, both in his plays and conversation. Ricketts was one of the few who could hold his own with Wilde. In his mid-twenties when he met Wilde, Ricketts did not appreciate that he was the most remarkable personality he was ever to encounter.

Though Ricketts designed most of Wilde's books, Aubrey Beardsley's designs for Wilde's *Salome* eclipsed his work. A brilliant draughtsman, Beardsley had set out to shock, and his illustrations succeeded in achieving the notoriety he also sought in his dress and conversation.

Of such sensationalism, Ricketts disapproved. For him, art was a high calling, to be followed with decorum and seriousness of purpose. More in keeping with this standard were the two women who wrote under the pseudonym "Michael Field." Katherine Bradley, the elder, was known as "Michael" while her niece, Edith Cooper, was called "Field." Their lives were dedicated to their poetry, verse plays and voluminous diaries. Ricketts designed many of their books. Though they (especially "Michael") could get on his nerves, Ricketts admired them for their noble devotion to their art and to each other.

Ricketts and Shannon's own relationship was similar. They had met as young art students. A French visitor commented that they lived "all for art." For Ricketts, art conferred the only immortality possible to man, and his whole life was given to creating it, to collecting it and to writing about it. Recognized as a connoisseur, he was offered the Directorship of the National Gallery in London, and later became artistic advisor to Canada's National Gallery. More important to him however, was his own work and Shannon's. Ricketts was a painter and sculptor, though his greatest achievements were in book and theatre design, Shannon, a painter and lithographer. Together they collected art of every genre and period: they acquired Egyptian antiquities, classical Greek pottery, sculpture and Tanagra figurines, works by Old Master, Pre-Raphaelite and other European artists, Japanese prints, Persian miniatures. Among their most prized possessions were works by the French Symbolist painter, Pierre Puvis de Chavannes, whom they considered the greatest artist of his age. Yet their means were always limited. In their youth, they went hungry to collect these objects.

Ricketts observed that his one perception of money was how to spend it wisely. He was no businessman. To avoid bankruptcy when he was a publisher of private press books, he needed the help of an able, practical manager, Charles Holmes, later Director of London's National Gallery. He always acknowledged how much he had learned from Ricketts, who had a passion for influencing people and guiding them to what he felt were correct artistic values.

United in their æsthetic creed, Ricketts and Shannon also complemented each other. While Ricketts scintillated in conversation, the quiet Shannon was known for good sense and judgement. Witty, erudite and extremely generous, Ricketts had had a difficult and unstable beginning in life, and could also be touchy and volatile. Having spent much of his youth moving about Europe, he was orphaned at a young age. With little formal education before art school, he had never been formed in any conventional mould. His responses to art and to life's difficulties were not cerebral, but highly visceral. For him, the world was full of "enemies," like the art critic Roger Fry, and anyone else who did not share his conservative views on art. Shannon, on the other hand, the son of a Lincolnshire country parson, had been brought up in a large family, and had a sunny, grounded disposition. One friend commented that if Ricketts had not met Shannon, he would have been the same, but if Shannon had never met Ricketts, his life would have been entirely different. Another close friend remarked that theirs was "the most marvellous human relationship" he had ever seen.

Yet it had its tensions. Shannon's work is full of sensuous images of women, of mothers with their children; he fell in love with women; he wanted to get married. For Ricketts, whose fragile security was rooted in Shannon's solid companionship, this was unthinkable. Besides, how could their collection be divided? When tragedy struck, Ricketts was forced to choose between maintaining their collection and selling it in the interest of the one person he really loved.

—J.G.P. Delaney

"The difference between the artist and the common man lies greatly in memory, combined with faculty of association. A common man's memory is a series of isolated facts. The artist links and chains them up whilst visualising them."
—Charles Ricketts, 3 April 1929

— • —

"This [painting] is how one pictures the angel of history: his face is turned toward the past. Where we perceive a chain of events, he sees one single catastrophe which keeps piling wreckage upon wreckage and hurls it in front of his feet. The angel would like to stay, awaken the dead and make whole what has been smashed. But a storm is blowing from Paradise; it has got caught in his wings with such violence that the angel can no longer close them. This storm irresistibly propels him into the future to which his back is turned, while the pile of debris before him grows skyward. This storm is what we call progress."
—Walter Benjamin, 1940

— • —

"Lives devoted to beauty usually end badly."
— Kenneth Clark

Last Romantics was first presented by Necessary Angel Theatre Company and The National Arts Centre, premiering at the Berkeley Street Theatre Downstairs, Toronto, Ontario, February 2003 with the following company:

Charles Holmes/	
Eric Brown	Jonathan Crombie
Charles Shannon	Oliver Dennis
Katherine Bradley	Barbara Gordon
Puvis de Chavannes/	
Oscar Wilde/	
Mackenzie King	Michael Hanrahan
Edith Cooper	Kate Hennig
Aubrey Beardsley/	
Thomas Martin	Steven McCarthy
Hetty Bruce/	
Hélène Cornèlie Ricketts	Vickie Papavs
Charles Ricketts	Julian Richings

Directed by Richard Rose
Set and Costume Design: Charlotte Dean
Lighting Design: Martin Conboy
Sound Design / Music: Marc Desormeaux
Stage Manager: Rebecca Miller
Production Manager: Simon Clemo
Assistant Director: Kathryn MacKay
Assistant Stage Manager: Fiona Kennedy
Assistant to the Director: Melissa Holler
Wardrobe Co-ordinator: Mary-Jo Carter Dodd
Set and Costume Design Assistant: April Viczko
Wardrobe Assistant: Erika Connor
Wigs: Jacqueline Robertson Cull

— • —

The production subsequently transferred to the National Arts Centre, Ottawa, Ontario, opening in April 2003.

— • —

The play was developed with the assistance of The Shaw Festival, National Arts Centre, Kingston University, Canadian Stage Company and Necessary Angel.

—•— Setting —•—

London and Ottawa, 1882-1937. Sticklers will note that some dates have been altered. However, the basic course of events—and their causal relationships—are retained. A character's aging should be accomplished through voice and physicality.

It's not necessary for the audience to know when each scene takes place. That said, here are dates:

1.	1930 / 1929	10.	1885
2.	April 1895	11.	November 11, 1929
3.	1885	12.	1929
4-6.	1895	13.	New Years Eve, 1929
7.	1930	14.	October 2, 1882
8-9.	1929	15.	1930

The characters are all based in fact. Ricketts's various encounters with Puvis de Chavannes, Martin, Wilde and Mackenzie King did in fact take place. Liberties have been taken. The real-life personages of Kathleen Bruce and Hetty Deacon were amalgamated. I have opted for the name "Hetty" so as to prevent her being confused with Katherine Bradley. The two women who make up the pseudonym "Michael Field" are not an exaggeration. They were arch anachronisms and should be played as such. Published by the Eragny Press of Lucien Pissarro (son of the painter Camille), *Whym Chow: Flame of Love* is one of the rarest and most bizarre books of its time.

Among the Charleses and the Fields, "Fay," Poets" and "Painters" are terms of address.

—•— Guide to Reading Line Endings —•—

...   Line fades.
–   Line interrupted by following line.
/   Line interrupted by following line at slash insertion point.
        (Does not apply to slashes in poetry quotations.)

Dialogue in parentheses indicate speech in a world separate from the rest of the action on stage.

Characters may interrupt and talk over Shannon's Act Two ramblings.

Most scenes benefit from a crisp, rapid delivery of lines.

— • — Notes on the Staging — • —

The set may be conceived as a wall of paintings accompanied by a movable ladder. Some natural element (suggestive of a tree or its leaves) may encroach. The sense of height and of being dwarfed by the artwork seems important. Other than various sculptures and *objets d'art*, the room itself can be sparsely furnished, allowing the set to become various locations. We should be permitted to see the joinery between scenes, actors themselves changing scenes at a fluid, even boisterous pace.

For variety's sake, the "wall" of paintings may be reconceived in various ways throughout the play. It is intended to be the unifying image: most scenes involve the paintings (or ladder) in some way. It is not necessary actually to render any paintings. In fact, it is probably preferable to suggest them only through the use of empty frames.

The room is a mind, a memory. Anything to support this suggestion, such as a seamless treatment of time and felicitous transformation of set objects in various scenes, is encouraged.

—•— Characters —•—

Charles Ricketts (b. 1866) Stooped, high reedy voice, flamboyant.
Charles Shannon (b. 1863) Tall, well-built, reserved.
Katherine Bradley Known as "Michael." Stout, ruddy, strong-willed. Ricketts's contemporary.
Edith Cooper Known as "Field." Katherine's niece and life-long companion.
Aubrey Beardsley Gaunt dandy, celebrated illustrator, and *enfant terrible*.
Hetty Bruce Shannon's friend and model, younger than him.
Charles Holmes Handsome protégé of Ricketts.

Puvis de Chavannes Forgotten French painter.
Oscar Wilde Vilified, broken writer.
William Lyon Mackenzie King Prime Minister of Canada.

Gallery Attendant
Thomas Martin Prison warder.
Eric Brown Canadian. Director of the National Gallery of Canada.
Hélène Cornèlie Ricketts Charles Ricketts's mother, dead.
Hangers, **Travellers**, **Gallery-Goers** and **Workers** should be cross-cast as required.

Cross-casting:
Best to cast with eight (five men, three women).
1. M   Ricketts
2. M   Shannon
3. F   Katherine
4. F   Edith
5. M   Beardsley, Gallery Attendant, Thomas Martin
6. F   Hetty, Hélène
7. M   Holmes, Brown
8. M   Oscar Wilde, Puvis de Chavannes, Mackenzie King

Last Romantics

—•— Act One —•—

I.

A blank wall, a few old paintings litter the room. A foot-high terracotta figurine (Tanagra) of a stout child sits forgotten. Two or three journals are piled somewhere. Worn and frail, Charles SHANNON eats from a wooden bowl.

SHANNON   They're taking away the art. Beauty will be wrung into money on which I'm expected to live. I wonder, am I worth the sacrifice? I get nervous when paintings are off their hooks; they seem so vulnerable, to time and other accidents. Worse is what's left behind: Naked walls! More indecent than the nude gods we hung on them. Their auras remain here... and here. You can only imagine.

EDITH blusters through, tidying. She packs the Tanagra into a box.

EDITH   Who are you chattering at.

SHANNON   The future.

EDITH   Oh, and you think they're listening?

SHANNON   I hope so.

EDITH   Well they're rather busy right now, carting off your Cranachs like so many ham hocks.

SHANNON   Who are?

EDITH   The movers, Charles. I tell you, this house has never seen such thick arms.

SHANNON grins, pointing at the wall behind him.

Well, perhaps framed on the walls, but that
doesn't count.

SHANNON   Yes it does.

EDITH   I shall humour you, Charles, only because these
are your last hours here. Enjoy them.

*EDITH exits. Four HANGERS swirl in,
transforming the wall as they hang splendid frames.*

SHANNON   You don't know who I am. Don't worry, I forgot
too for a while. I look ahead now, to you, the
future. You're my last, best creation – mute,
impatient, waiting to judge me. To start: I am
Charles Shannon.

*Charles RICKETTS, elderly but vital, swirls in
supervising the hanging of paintings.*

RICKETTS   Too high!

(SHANNON   I present Charles Ricketts.)

RICKETTS   It's Venus! Botticelli never wanted us to grovel at
her feet.

(SHANNON   I met him when he was sixteen and up a tree.)

RICKETTS   She's painted so you might look beauty in the eye.

(SHANNON   I was eighteen, in a considerably safer location.)

HOLMES enters RICKETTS's world.

HOLMES   Ricketts...

RICKETTS   Holmes! Truth and beauty!

HOLMES   Let the men go, Ricketts. It's New Year's Eve.

RICKETTS   And you open tomorrow.

(SHANNON   London's Italian Exhibition, the largest ever.)

RICKETTS   Do you want the eyes of the future admiring blank walls?

HOLMES   The men'll be back by sunrise.

RICKETTS   Ha! Precisely when they'll be staggering into bed.

HOLMES   They have families waiting for them.

RICKETTS   Go then, go chew geese with your wives.

> *The HANGERS clear out, nodding thanks.*
> *SHANNON continues to the audience.*

HOLMES   You look awful. I knew this was too much for you.

RICKETTS   I'll rest soon enough, dear boy. Look. A wall of Botticellis, never in the same room before. Even the artist himself never saw what we now see.

HOLMES   There are certain advantages to the Twentieth Century after all.

RICKETTS   I wouldn't go *that* far. Now leave. I'll hang this Piero myself.

(SHANNON   Piero, the great forgotten painter of myths.)

RICKETTS   Then I'll take Shannon home.

(SHANNON   Forgotten while Botticelli is remembered.)

HOLMES   Happy New Year.

(SHANNON   Why is that?)

RICKETTS   My regards to your wife.

(SHANNON   Why do we love one thing and not another?)

> *The others leave. SHANNON climbs the ladder*
> *with the bowl. He admires a view.*

I'm telling this wrong. I've started at the end. Patience, please: this bowl is my mind, as easily drained as it was filled. I stand as close to you as I dare: close to you, the future, the one place we never looked. I see you looking back at me, the past, wondering why you should care. The meagre past. It's where Ricketts and I always wanted to be, even when we were young. When so much... so much was new.

> *He drops the bowl. As it smacks the floor, lights shift. He turns to a painting on the wall beside him. Furniture inhabits the room. Apples are bowled along the floor into the room.*

2.

> *SHANNON is up the ladder hanging the painting. It's not an easy reach.*

RICKETTS   (*offstage*) Shannon? Where are you?

SHANNON   Drawing room! How was your day at the galleries?

RICKETTS   (*offstage*) Holbein improved enormously. Titian, as usual, was captivating.

SHANNON   Well he captivated for too long. We have guests here any–

RICKETTS   (*offstage*) I know, I know, the tea-fight. Where are you?

SHANNON   I'm hanging the Shepherdess.

RICKETTS   (*offstage*) No! Wait! I wanted to–

SHANNON   Done.

> *RICKETTS comes storming into the room, his arms full of lettuce heads. He stops.*

RICKETTS   Too high.

SHANNON	Where else could I–
RICKETTS	Down here with the Watteau, of course.
SHANNON	(*descending*) Millet would hardly consort with Watteau.
RICKETTS	Then their proximity will spark a stormy *rapprochement*.
SHANNON	Well, not tonight.
RICKETTS	There you go, Chubbs, holding off the inevitable. Wherefore the apples?
SHANNON	Oh, I dropped the hammer and it struck–
RICKETTS	The bowl? No. (*madly searching*) Not the Adam's bowl...
SHANNON	No, just a, a humble wooden one.
RICKETTS	(*finding it, collapsing in extravagant relief*) Well be careful! If anything were to happen...
SHANNON	Nothing *did* happen.

> *SHANNON helps him up, a playful flirtation which RICKETTS interrupts, biting an apple.*

RICKETTS	Blech. You bruised them. Away. Banished. Nothing but beautiful things tonight.

> *RICKETTS flits about arranging the lettuce heads in bowls with sprays of flowers. At ease, they move about their familiar preparations.*

After the past week of horrors our guests crave reassurance. Which reminds me: we must compliment Michael: she found the secret to perpetual youth.

SHANNON	Oh! And in just the nick of time.

RICKETTS   A chemist in Wells concocted an elixir: radium
                 deftly mixed with silver ashes.

SHANNON   You believe this?

RICKETTS   He was ninety-eight! Would've lived forever had
                 he not fallen off a bicycle.

SHANNON   Sounds dreadfully unsafe.

RICKETTS   Haven't I always said that about bicycles?

SHANNON   The noxious application.

RICKETTS   Oh – entirely safe. After the first phase, which
                 turns the skin black.

SHANNON   Good God...

RICKETTS   But when that layer falls, one sheds all physical
                 and moral blemishes and becomes as imperishable
                 as Lillie Langtry. (*prancing about*) Can you see me?
                 A glory of curls clustered on my crown like goats
                 grazing the brows of a once-barren hill? Shannon?
                 What's wrong?

SHANNON   (*of the painting*) I waited as long as I dared. If you'd
                 come back earlier...

RICKETTS   Not at all. It looks lovely. It does. I like it up
                 there. Mm.

                 A moment of gentle stillness. Together affectionately,
                 they admire their paintings.

SHANNON   It is too high.

RICKETTS   Why do you say that?

SHANNON   Because it is.

RICKETTS   Nonsense.

SHANNON   You were right.

RICKETTS   *I* don't think I'm right, why should you? You're only doing this to–

SHANNON   Really. I find this painting too high on the wall.

RICKETTS   No you don't.

SHANNON   Yes I do.

RICKETTS   Fine. Suit yourself. Paint much today?

SHANNON   Yes. Had Hetty in to sit for me. Go take a look.

RICKETTS   Mine eyes are full at present. Any regrets?

SHANNON   Mm?

RICKETTS   From our guests. Any regrets.

SHANNON   None. Actually, no post today.

RICKETTS   Curious. Is she coming?

SHANNON   I expect so.

RICKETTS   Well. Here, let me...

SHANNON   (*hanging it*) There.

RICKETTS   Well, Chubbers, you were right. It *is* much better down here after all.

> *SHANNON turns to look at him, a shared smile. They are interrupted by clomping, off.*

KATHERINE & EDITH   (*offstage*) Painters!

RICKETTS & SHANNON   Early. (*beat*) Poets!

> *KATHERINE and EDITH waft in.*

KATHERINE   Propelled by tragedy, we are come early.

SHANNON	No...
EDITH	No?
RICKETTS	Yes. You are early. But come in anyway.
EDITH	(*kiss*) Charles, you hermit. Since our last at-home, you have remained obstinately unheard, unseen...
KATHERINE	And thus, unloved.
SHANNON	I've been painting.
RICKETTS	And spending! We bought a new canvas and paid the deposit on a charming Tanagra. He is thus short funds for a postage stamp.
SHANNON	(*kissing KATHERINE*) Michael, your face has a Tuscan quality of radiance.
KATHERINE	You think so?
SHANNON	Yes. Have you been washing in radium?
EDITH	(*swatting RICKETTS*) You were not to tell!
KATHERINE	Fay, you are wicked. This is the debut of my new visage – you must immediately forget the circumstances of its arrival, or I shall leave.
RICKETTS	Righteous Indignation is the most dangerous of your deadly virtues.
EDITH	Michael, we do have more important concerns.
KATHERINE	Quite right, Field. We come heralding cataclysm.
EDITH	As our dearest friends, we wanted you to learn the news.
SHANNON	We have news too – look at our new painting.
KATHERINE	I rather think ours is a more pressing–

RICKETTS	Just look!
KATHERINE	Ahh? Ahh. Wonderful.
EDITH	Enchanting. Now if we might reciprocate...
SHANNON	No, this one. A new Millet. A shepherdess.
EDITH	Mm. A perfect addition to the burgeoning collection.
KATHERINE	An exquisite piece of tranquillity.

And with that, Aubrey BEARDSLEY enters.

RICKETTS	While it lasted.
EDITH	Oh dear, this evening is starting dreadfully.
BEARDSLEY	Clapping eyes on you, I'd have to concur.
KATHERINE	Sir, she didn't mean...
EDITH	It is only that we had something to say–
BEARDSLEY	And it will now be heard by a person of consequence. So this is the celebrated Ricketts-Shannon home. I see I have come too early.
RICKETTS	Ah Beardsley, always imagining yourself ahead of your time.
BEARDSLEY	Better than lagging forgotten in the dust.
SHANNON	Aubrey Beardsley, may I present–
BEARDSLEY	Yes, yes. Is Oscar here? Your front door is wide open.
RICKETTS	We expect forty guests. If the door were closed, we'd spend all evening answering it.
BEARDSLEY	The draught will not be good for me; I caught cold last night.

KATHERINE   Oh dear. How?

BEARDSLEY   I foolishly went walking without the tassel on my cane. A properly placed servant would ensure a sealed house.

RICKETTS   Young man, to keep servants is to buy less art.

BEARDSLEY   Old man, you have strange priorities.

RICKETTS   I am not old.

EDITH   Thanks to their frugality, Mister Beardsley, these two men have assembled what is fast becoming the most remarkable private collection in England.

BEARDSLEY   (*gesturing guest-wards*) Yet I see it suffers from a preoccupation with antiquities.

EDITH   Mister Beardsley, that's enough of your, your...

KATHERINE   Your bony, debonair impudence!

> *BEARDSLEY turns to fix these women with a look. SHANNON affects a* détente.

SHANNON   I present our dear friends Katherine Bradley and her niece, Edith Cooper.

EDITH   We are also known as (*indicating KATHERINE*) Michael (*indicating herself*) Field.

BEARDSLEY   You? Michael Field? The playwright?

KATHERINE   Alas, yes.

BEARDSLEY   Why "alas?"

KATHERINE   Because now that you know our secret, we shall have to cut out your tongue.

BEARDSLEY   How theatrical!

RICKETTS   Perhaps best served on a platter like the head of John the Baptist.

EDITH   As did George Eliot and the Brontë sisters, we publish pseudonymously.

BEARDSLEY   Such traversals of gender fascinate me.

RICKETTS   We'd have never guessed.

BEARDSLEY   When am I to see one of your plays?

KATHERINE   They are verse tragedies, to be read.

RICKETTS   In exceedingly handsome books.

EDITH   Charles has illustrated and published some of our titles.

RICKETTS   Which you'd know if you actually *read*.

BEARDSLEY   I am too busy with commissions and parties. Besides, to have read a book rather clutters one's opinion of it.

RICKETTS   A strange thing for a book illustrator to say.

BEARDSLEY   My drawings relieve the drudgery of print. I say, are you expecting rabbits?

RICKETTS   They are a decoration.

EDITH   Emerald roses.

BEARDSLEY   A most curious ornament.

RICKETTS   Have you ever looked closely at a lettuce?

BEARDSLEY   Only if examining for beetles on my plate.

RICKETTS   I wonder if you have a skin over your eyes, not unlike a kind of lizard I once saw on my travels to Egypt. Peel it back and you might learn to see beauty.

BEARDSLEY	I shudder to think what Oscar would say.
SHANNON	Oscar adores them.
BEARDSLEY	Oh? Perhaps he'll arrive with one in his buttonhole.
SHANNON	If he ever arrives.
BEARDSLEY	Yes.
RICKETTS	Yes...

A long pause.

EDITH	Has there been any news?
BEARDSLEY	Of course there is news. Every day there is news.
KATHERINE	*We* have news!
EDITH	Yes. It involves my father.
SHANNON	People underestimate the danger he's in.
EDITH	My father?
RICKETTS, BEARDSLEY & SHANNON	Oscar!
BEARDSLEY	As Degas said, so much taste will lead to prison.
KATHERINE	Let them exhaust themselves.
RICKETTS	Degas is a git. The Crown wouldn't dare prosecute. They'd destroy everything beautiful and right and just about the last ten years of art in this country.
BEARDSLEY	I must concur.
EDITH	Still, such unbridled pursuit of pleasure must have its consequence...

RICKETTS   I'm not talking about pleasure. I'm talking about the obvious progression of art.

BEARDSLEY   You know, I think I'll call 'round his hotel–

RICKETTS   No you won't. He's assured me that despite everything he will be in attendance tonight. He rarely misses our Thursdays.

SHANNON   He says ours was the one place in London where one will never be bored.

BEARDSLEY   I must disabuse him of that notion.

RICKETTS   You know, Oscar visited us the very night he received that insult from Bosie's father – the accusation that started the trial. He gazed out that window at the last of the sun and sighed:

SHANNON   "I live in a world of puppets,"

RICKETTS   He said,

SHANNON   "Who do not understand, and yet would play with the strings."

BEARDSLEY   Prophetic.

SHANNON   Tragic, really.

A pause.

RICKETTS   Where is everyone?

KATHERINE   Speaking of tragedies, gentlemen...

EDITH   Yes.

SHANNON   Yes. You had news.

BEARDSLEY   Yes.

KATHERINE   Yes. Well? How to begin...

They are interrupted by a bang offstage, whispered cursing. They become agitated, expectant.

EDITH Wait.

SHANNON Here he is now.

RICKETTS I detect his footfall.

EDITH And I, his *eau de toilette*.

KATHERINE We once received a letter by him. It was redolent with his scent.

BEARDSLEY Shh!

All stand with bated breath. HETTY enters the room. She is surprised to find all eyes on her.

HETTY Oh! My apologies. I thought there was a party...

BEARDSLEY You're not the only one.

SHANNON Miss Bruce, uh, please, come in...

HETTY The door, it was–

BEARDSLEY The door is unmanned so the room may be filled. Certainly with wind and art. With guests? Disputably.

HETTY Oh! Sir, you are... are you...

BEARDSLEY (*flirting*) Yes. Yes, I am.

SHANNON Come in, Miss Bruce.

HETTY (*gritted teeth*) Introduce me, Charles.

RICKETTS Yes, "Charles." You're quite thoughtless, from shampooing your head last night.

SHANNON Hetty Bruce, meet our dear friends Michael and Field.

HETTY   What curious names...

RICKETTS   Hetty is Shannon's current painter's model. Evidently, also not a reader.

HETTY   I know you, Mister Beardsley. I have admired your drawings for some time.

BEARDSLEY   I admired *you* in Shannon's canvas at the Royal Academy.

HETTY   It won a medal.

SHANNON   He knows that.

BEARDSLEY   Humility is tiresome and only slows conversation.

EDITH   What is the painting called?

SHANNON   "The Morning Toilet."

KATHERINE   Has it sold?

RICKETTS   Not with a title like that.

> *HETTY laughs a good long laugh. The others watch astonished, RICKETTS with barely concealed revulsion.*

SHANNON   Would you care to sit?

HETTY   Why – you're not painting me.

BEARDSLEY   (*continuing with RICKETTS*) I thought the canvas commendable but rather old-fashioned. Frankly, it looked as out of place as an Old Master painting.

HETTY   (*to SHANNON*) It's exhausting, keeping still all day.

RICKETTS   (*to BEARDSLEY*) We take that as a compliment.

BEARDSLEY   You would, lumbering around here like Raphael incarnate.

RICKETTS   If I am such an anachronism, Beardsley, why have you brazenly plagiarised my style?

SHANNON   Ricketts please, not now...

BEARDSLEY   (*to RICKETTS*) My good man, you are vaguely delusional.

KATHERINE   You must admit, sir, there is a similarity.

EDITH   Everyone says so.

BEARDSLEY   Why steal what no one will buy? Your paintings gather dust. Your books can't sell a hundred copies while my illustration of Oscar's *Salome* made me rich and exceedingly famous!

RICKETTS   Attention is not admiration, Beardsley. You will learn that one day.

SHANNON   (*beat*) Ricketts always speaks his mind.

RICKETTS   Hardly. On some occasions, the truth is far too precious to waste.

HETTY   Then what do you say?

RICKETTS   When.

HETTY   When you see a painting you loathe, but don't want to "waste truth?"

KATHERINE   He pronounces it "novel."

HETTY   (*chuckling*) Novel...

SHANNON   Hetty...

HETTY   Go away.

BEARDSLEY   Miss Bruce is right – what's wrong with novelty?

RICKETTS   Novelty alone is valueless. Beauty and the art expressing it has centuries behind it.

BEARDSLEY Except I'm erecting a wholly new conception of beauty.

RICKETTS Impossible.

BEARDSLEY Today's artist has a new way of seeing. You may hate it, but you can't ignore it.

RICKETTS I pity it, and so will posterity. Since the first barbarian scratched a pattern on bone, art has aimed at being permanent, not new.

BEARDSLEY Ah, is that why your paintings all look like muddy Italian forgeries?

KATHERINE Mister Beardsley, there's no need to insult–

RICKETTS You are nothing but a petulant anarchist who would destroy what he cannot change.

EDITH Gentlemen...

BEARDSLEY The public like my work. It is extremely popular. They don't like yours. You are, what, thirty years old, but you paint—and walk—like an old man.

RICKETTS I am notoriously young and slim for my age! I'm told I've found the secret of youth.

SHANNON Or a stash of radium.

> *RICKETTS swats him. BEARDSLEY zones in on SHANNON.*

BEARDSLEY Mister Shannon? What do you think?

SHANNON About what.

BEARDSLEY About the merits of your æsthetic.

SHANNON I... uh... well. Ricketts and I are of the same mind.

RICKETTS	And at odds with the throngs of ignorant Philistines.
EDITH	Speaking of throngs, we have news we should like to share before they arrive.
BEARDSLEY	Take your time. Clearly, some other event has claimed the cream.
EDITH	We learned today an awful truth.
BEARDSLEY	The only kind.
KATHERINE	Gentlemen. We are assured the front page of tomorrow's *Times*.
HETTY	Wonderful!
KATHERINE	Alas, no. They have finally found my brother.
EDITH	And my father.
SHANNON	Oh no.
EDITH	(*to BEARDSLEY*) One and the same man, lost three months ago in Switzerland.
KATHERINE	On a hiking trip.
EDITH	And now found. Dead.
BEARDSLEY	Oh!
RICKETTS	Stop.
BEARDSLEY	Why, because it verges on interesting?
RICKETTS	I don't want to hear this.
KATHERINE	Fay, you are nervous and therefore tactless.
RICKETTS	Here, now, in this room... it's bad luck and extremely uncouth.

SHANNON   Ricketts. Why don't you arrange the punch. Go.

                After a silent beat, RICKETTS storms out.

                Ladies, I'm sorry. Our condolences. His own
                mother died young; can't bear talk of death.

HETTY   I can.

KATHERINE   The event, while tragic, has at last disposed of our
                theories of my brother being marauded by gypsies
                for his pocket watch, or drowned in the Visp.

EDITH   Instead, he lost his way, struck his head and,
                beyond reach of help, perished in the forest.

KATHERINE   Two wood-cutters found him, untouched. If
                somewhat decomposed.

BEARDSLEY   I expect he was an earthy man.

KATHERINE   He loved nature, yes. And now the mystery
                shrouding his disappearance is solved.

HETTY   But it has only opened more questions!

EDITH   I beg your pardon?

HETTY   Well? Why was his hike so remote? Did he fall or
                was he pushed? How long was he alive? Did his
                moans frighten shepherds who might have saved
                him? Ladies, don't you wonder?

SHANNON   No, Hetty, they don't. Why seek where you may
                not find?

HETTY   I'm only saying that one can never take the
                measure of an adventurous man.

KATHERINE   We are assuaged. We have ceased the hunt. You
                don't know–

HETTY   But I *do* know, very well. I confess a fascination
                with heroic men. They're the only ones who

accomplish anything of consequence. Your brother sounds like such a man.

EDITH   A kind thing to say, Miss Bruce.

> *RICKETTS enters with the punch and stands, listening.*

HETTY   Like all adventurous men who perish doing adventurous things, he will always be dead and yet curiously still living. One hears about the death, yes, but one doesn't really believe it. In your mind he's still clinging to that mountainside. Clinging to life, to hope, his fingers scrabbling in the gravel like desperate worms. It's a kind of living death: he's not here but he never properly left. In a way, he achieved a kind of immortality. (*The others gape a moment.*) See, I've been looking for such a man myself.

KATHERINE   What for?

HETTY   For my children, the necessary heroic stock.

BEARDSLEY   Oo goody. And are you still looking?

HETTY   No. But he has yet to propose.

SHANNON   Punch?

RICKETTS   I admire your restraint, Miss Bruce.

> *The offstage door slams. All stop. Someone is heard running. Bated breath.*

HETTY   Him?

RICKETTS & BEARDSLEY   No.

SHANNON   Oscar never runs.

> *Puffing, HOLMES enters. Young.*

HOLMES   Sir...

RICKETTS   (*clasping him*) Holmes! You're just what we need right now.

HOLMES   Sir...

RICKETTS   Holmes, you know Misses Bradley and Cooper. And Aubrey Beardsley, the illustrator who has stolen my style and eclipsed my success...

HOLMES   Do you have a moment–

SHANNON   And this is Miss Bruce–

RICKETTS   Punch?

HOLMES   Sir, I must talk to you about some serious business.

RICKETTS   Holmes is our manager at Vale Press.

HOLMES   Mister Ricketts, may I–

RICKETTS   Lovely boy. Rotten artist, but good business / sense–

SHANNON   Shut it, Ricketts! What do you need?

HOLMES   Well? Money.

RICKETTS   We're hardly flush. We just bought a Millet and placed a deposit on the–

SHANNON   What do you need it for?

HOLMES   Oscar.

BEARDSLEY (*pause*) What.

HOLMES   Bail.

SHANNON   Oh God.

BEARDSLEY	No.
EDITH	No.
KATHERINE	I knew it.
RICKETTS	What happened. Holmes.
HOLMES	It seems that, well... Mister Wilde was just arrested.

Lights change. SHANNON addresses the audience.

RICKETTS	The day is dying.
(SHANNON	He invented our world.)
RICKETTS	Fading to nothing. But what rapturous death. See Titian's ripe clouds?
(SHANNON	Blind to what hurt him.)
RICKETTS	The smudge of a Turner horizon? Do you see?
(SHANNON	Blind.)
RICKETTS	How much hope we once held.
(SHANNON	He ruined everything.)

Lights and sound shift back to the room. RICKETTS paces, cleaning up. SHANNON looks out the window. KATHERINE and EDITH cuddle together on the sofa. The others left long ago.

KATHERINE	Stupid fool, pushing his luck like that.
EDITH	It's as if he *wanted* it to happen.
RICKETTS	Hardly. Oscar told me here, in this room, he'd let the accusation pass, avoid conflict at all costs. So why did he foolishly court disaster?

KATHERINE	That nasty paramour of his Bosie put him up to it.
RICKETTS	He looked out that window at the last of the sun. Watched a man in the street selling sausage rolls.
KATHERINE	I'm cramping. Ooo. There.
RICKETTS	He turned to me with his gentle, jowly smile and said... Shannon? (*pause*) He said, "What curious things people will eat." I replied, "Oscar, I suppose they must be hungry."
EDITH	Better?
KATHERINE	There. Yes. Thanks, duck.
RICKETTS	I'll arrange a committee.
KATHERINE	You'd do well to keep your distance.
RICKETTS	That's out of the question.
EDITH	Distance does seem cruel, Michael.
KATHERINE	One must maintain a distinction between Mister Wilde and people like, like... well. Fay and Charles aren't at all like him.
RICKETTS	Oscar has been persecuted by a jealous and Philistine society which hates art and loathes the artist. You'll see: the men of England will rise to his defence.
SHANNON	Oscar's "defence" just took the night boat to Calais.
RICKETTS	*We* didn't. (*pause, watching SHANNON look out the window*) From where you stand, Shannon, there are infinitely more interesting things to be viewing.
SHANNON	I should have seen her home.

RICKETTS	Yes, well I'm sure the streets have never been safer.
KATHERINE	On the contrary, I expect they are choked with men desperate to prove their virility.
RICKETTS	Why did you bring her here anyway?
SHANNON	She's a friend.
RICKETTS	She's your model!
SHANNON	Considering tonight's honoured visitant was just arrested for gross indecency, I hardly think a model in the room proves a disgrace–
RICKETTS	He's your friend too.
SHANNON	We know what trouble he got into with those boys. The police can obviously prove it. That's why they arrested him. He's ruined.
EDITH	What, you think he'll go to jail?
SHANNON	He's *in* jail.
RICKETTS	Oscar cannot be ruined. He is too great a man.
SHANNON	The public hate him, don't you see? Not just for having relations with those young men, but for... well, for daring to show them their own crudeness and ignorance.

> *RICKETTS scoffs, exasperated, and continues picking up his lettuces. KATHERINE gives a sudden gasp and a tortured look to EDITH. RICKETTS rolls his eyes.*

KATHERINE	Do you know what this means?
RICKETTS	What.
KATHERINE	Mister Wilde will eclipse the placement of my brother's obituary.

EDITH   But we were assured front page!

SHANNON   Oh for the love of God...

KATHERINE   Well?

SHANNON   Do you understand what has happened here?

EDITH   Yes. Papa has been horribly upstaged.

SHANNON   It's over! The most brilliant and vociferous and convincing exponent of the æsthetic movement will be judged a pervert. The rest of us will be equated with his crimes. This will certainly ruin Beardsley.

RICKETTS   That's *one* good thing.

SHANNON   What an ugly man you are.

                   Pause.

DRIVER   (*offstage*) Halloooo...? (*pause*) Hallo?

KATHERINE   There's our cab. Coming!

EDITH   Gentlemen, as usual, a lovely evening...

KATHERINE   Yes, quite. It's nice to be at the centre of it all for once.

EDITH   Even peripherally.

RICKETTS   Close the front door behind you.

                   The women leave. RICKETTS and SHANNON alone.

                   Tomorrow. I shall work on the Daphnis and Chloe illustrations. You might take a look. I need to visit Legros' studio, help select work for his exhibition. His paintings tend to the sentimental and I shall weed those out, you can be sure.

Oh, and lunch with young Holmes. Do you think he'll still come round? (*pause*) Shannon? What will you do. Tomorrow.

SHANNON Paint.

RICKETTS Yes. Paint, good. I'll be in to have a look. Shannon.

They share a look across the room.

Do you... do you... like her? (*gesturing to the painting*) The new shepherdess?

SHANNON I don't know.

RICKETTS goes to the Millet. SHANNON elsewhere. Lights on him change.

SHANNON "Paint." Her. Him. Whomever. Put them in drapery and call them gods. We slapped paint on canvas. That was our job. We used an old technique which, like our subjects and style, had fallen totally out of fashion. It is called glazing and is very difficult. In glazing you apply translucent layers of paint, one on top of another, to try and create the appearance of one solid colour. It took months to finish a painting, and with so many opportunities for misjudging the various pigments or their order of application, it was easy to make mistakes. But when the effect works—when the colours seep through properly— it creates a kind of luminous memory on the canvas. It's as if something within the painting continues to live. It's as if, were one to delve through the dark top skin that time has soiled, one might find a lighter, still-gleaming soul within, from an earlier time, however faint.

3.

Train whistle. Station sounds. PEOPLE with luggage disembark and are greeted. On the platform, RICKETTS waits among them, impatient and distraught.

RICKETTS   Oh Shannon.

SHANNON   Ricketts?

RICKETTS   You made it.

SHANNON   The Channel was rough, nearly missed my train. And I certainly missed you.

RICKETTS   Stay away.

SHANNON   What's wrong?

RICKETTS   I'm dying at the tender age of nineteen!

SHANNON   No...

RICKETTS   Two days in Paris and I've been stricken with morbid pestilence.

SHANNON   Have you seen a doctor?

RICKETTS   Too late. It's some incurable affliction that struck Herod and other sinful wretches.

SHANNON   Now just calm–

RICKETTS   How can I? I woke covered in these awful bumps, my nightshirt flecked with blood!

SHANNON   Show me.

RICKETTS   No.

SHANNON   I'm not having my first trip to Paris ruined by your–

RICKETTS   Let go. I am hideous! Stop – Chunky, people are staring!

SHANNON   Lift up your shirt.

RICKETTS   (*pause*) I told you.

SHANNON   What kind of hotel did you get us?

RICKETTS   Not good enough for me to die in!

SHANNON   I should think not. You've got fleas.

RICKETTS   (*pause*) Fleas. No. This is much, much, much worse than fleas.

SHANNON   Come. We are finding a new hotel.

RICKETTS   Fleas? Really? Chunky, I thought I'd be dead ere I saw twenty years. I imagined you keeping vigil, like Severn nursed Keats.

SHANNON   New hotel, then the galleries.

RICKETTS   I feel I've had a miracle cure!

SHANNON   Just in time to show me the Louvre.

RICKETTS   Yes, the Louvre!

— • —

Their luggage whisked away, the space transforms into a gallery. VIEWERS drift through. SHANNON examines paintings in youthful awe. RICKETTS looks at SHANNON.

RICKETTS   Rooms and rooms of Old Masters.

SHANNON   How did they do it?

RICKETTS   Perfect technique, mythic subjects and a fleeting moment, brilliantly seized. Let these men be your teachers. And look. Great God, we have been given a sign.

> *They turn to look at an old man, PUVIS de
> Chavannes, wearing a huge cloak and regarding
> a painting. At the same time a somnambulant
> gallery ATTENDANT drifts through the room.*

ATTENDANT   *Nous fermons, veuillez je vous prie regagner la sortie.*

SHANNON   What.

RICKETTS   You know who that is?

SHANNON   ...No?

RICKETTS   Think. I've told you about him.

SHANNON   Who.

RICKETTS   The greatest living exponent of classical art.

SHANNON   Puvis de Chavannes?

RICKETTS   Yes!

SHANNON   That's him, there?

RICKETTS   Like us, seeking inspiration.

SHANNON   Come on.

RICKETTS   No! Chubbs, we can't just... go and *talk* to him.

SHANNON   Why not?

RICKETTS   I'd be crippled with timidity.

SHANNON   Then don't say anything.

ATTENDANT   (*passing through again*) *Nous fermons, s'il vous plaît...*

RICKETTS   But you don't speak French.

SHANNON   So?

RICKETTS   Shannon!

SHANNON   Come on.

                   *RICKETTS in tow, he approaches the man with
                   awed deference.*

SHANNON   *Excusez-moi, monsieur...*

PUVIS   *(Absorbed in the painting, he dismisses him with a
                   wave, mistaking him for the ATTENDANT.) Oui, je
                   sais. Donne une autre minute au vieillard.*

SHANNON   What's he saying?

RICKETTS   *(stepping in, very shy, in perfect French) Monsieur,
                   permettez-nous de rendre hommage á un grand artiste.*

SHANNON   What'd you say?

RICKETTS   Just bow!

PUVIS   *Je suis surpris que deux jeunes Anglais puissent
                   reconnaître ce peintre oublié.*

SHANNON   What'd he say.

RICKETTS   He's surprised we recognise him.

SHANNON   Tell him he is the greatest painter alive.

RICKETTS   *Monsieur, vous n'êtes pas oublié.*

ATTENDANT   *(passing through again) Mesieurs, je vous en prie...*

PUVIS   *Silence, ne vois-tu donc pas que ces deux jeunes hommes
                   sont venus ici en pélerinage?*

RICKETTS   *(scratching himself enthusiastically) Nous aussi, sommes
                   des artistes, Monsieur.*

PUVIS   *Mmm?*

SHANNON   What'd you say?

RICKETTS   *Vos conseils nous seraient précieux.*

SHANNON	Charles, what did you–
RICKETTS	I told him we want his advice.
SHANNON	*Oui! Oui! Monsieur!*
PUVIS	*Quel âge avez-vous?*
SHANNON	Oh – I know that one.... Ah, ah, ah, ah...
RICKETTS	*Moi, Monsieur, j'ai dix-neuf ans et mon ami en a vingt-deux.*
SHANNON	*...Vingt-deux. Exactement.*
PUVIS	*Ah, vous êtes des enfants terribles?*
SHANNON	*Oui! Oui! Terrible!*
	RICKETTS elbows him.
	Ow!
PUVIS	*Vous plairait-il de vous joindre à moi pour le dîner?*
RICKETTS	*Ce serait, Monsieur, nous faire un grand honneur.*
SHANNON	Where are we going?
RICKETTS	To sit at the feet of the master – come on!
	They whisk off after PUVIS, leaving the gallery ATTENDANT to shrug.

— • —

	Bedroom. RICKETTS and SHANNON are immediately wheeled back on in the bed. Giddy from their day, they wrestle playfully in and under a mound of blankets and pillows.
SHANNON	*(imitating PUVIS, but with a bad accent)* "Quelle charmante jeunesse."

RICKETTS   What a dinner!

SHANNON   I'm stuffed.

RICKETTS   With oysters and ambition. You heard what he said.

SHANNON   It was in *French*!

RICKETTS   You'll follow in his footsteps.

SHANNON   I will?

RICKETTS   You saw beauty where others see only a dull, cracked canvas.

SHANNON   I did, didn't I.

RICKETTS   Thus spake the master: Go home to paint the subjects of antiquity, of allegory.

SHANNON   The old æsthetics, *très charmante*.

RICKETTS   You will study...

SHANNON   And paint...

RICKETTS   And submit your work only to me for criticism.

SHANNON   Then emerge the master, complete and undeniable...

RICKETTS   Upon whose princely income I will live...

SHANNON   *We* will live...

RICKETTS   For the rest of our lives.

SHANNON   But meanwhile...

RICKETTS   I will take the burden for our immediate wants.

SHANNON   You will draw ads...

RICKETTS	And illustrate books, anything...
SHANNON	Anything...
RICKETTS	Anything for an income.
SHANNON	Do you think it will work?
RICKETTS	Charles Shannon, did I not tell you the day we met that you were cut out for greatness? Now be a dear and scratch me.
SHANNON	You glad I made you talk to him?
RICKETTS	Yes!
SHANNON	You glad I got us a new hotel?
RICKETTS	I'd be dying pallid and bloodless without you.
SHANNON	You glad to be a *charmante jeunesse*?
RICKETTS	Oh Shannon, yes, scratch me! Yes! Ah! Ah! Ah! (*beat*) Ahhhhh.
SHANNON	What?
RICKETTS	I'm bleeding.

> *RICKETTS runs offstage. SHANNON gets out of bed. He considers the bedsheets, then begins to arrange them.*

SHANNON	*Charmante.* I need you, Hetty. Please.

4.

> *HETTY appears naked from within the bedsheets. SHANNON arranges a sheet over her left shoulder. Swathed in drapery, she unabashedly exposes her right torso and breast. He hands her an arrow which she holds against her chest, arranges apples beside her, and begins to paint.*

HETTY   Ohhh? I'm spent.

SHANNON   Sit as you were before. There. *Charmante*.

HETTY   So I heard about Mister Wilde: two years hard labour.

SHANNON   The harlots danced in the street.

HETTY   Well, even prostitutes recognise a moral victory.

SHANNON   It was a business victory, Hetty. Now the rent boys are scared off their corners, the girls have seen their competition eliminated. Hardly a return to decency.

HETTY   What, you're defending him?

SHANNON   You never met him.

HETTY   No, missed my chance at your party. But the more I hear about Mister Wilde, the less sad I am the coppers nabbed him. Even that scrawny disciple of his Tawdry Beardless smears him.

SHANNON   Well. You're tapped in, aren't you.

HETTY   You're not the only artist I model for.

SHANNON   Although I do enjoy certain exclusive privileges.

HETTY   Yes, and thanks to me you'll be fashionable for the first time in your life.

SHANNON   You think so.

HETTY   Oh yes. Marriage is exceedingly fashionable right now.

        SHANNON gives HETTY a lengthy kiss.

        What are you making of me?

SHANNON   A wounded Amazon.

HETTY   Ooo! And where am I wounded?

SHANNON   Blood would distract from your beauty.

HETTY   I'm pretty cheeky about showing the rest of my anatomy.

SHANNON   Yes, you're a warrior who's elected to ignore her requisite surgical ceremony.

HETTY   What does *that* mean?

SHANNON   It means you didn't chop your titty off.

HETTY   Eeeee! They did that?

SHANNON   (*miming*) So they could shoot the bow properly.

HETTY   The things people were capable of.

SHANNON   It's just what they did. They wouldn't have thought it remarkable. (*painting*) Chin down.

HETTY   But you are, excavating the past, showing us where we come from.

SHANNON   I'm just painting. Chin.

HETTY   And years from now, people will see: "Charles Shannon's first great works were of the woman he married." They'll marvel that people were ever so beautiful. They'll look to your paintings, Charles, for a glimpse of our perfect love, the love between an artist and his muse.

SHANNON   Hetty...

HETTY   Yes, yes, my bloody flipping chin. Why am I posed with apples?

SHANNON   A painter doesn't explain his own canvas.

HETTY   I know who does. (*picks one up*) Smells musty and old, reminds me of someone.

SHANNON	Hetty...
HETTY	Smell it!
SHANNON	He is an excellent critic.
HETTY	Good for stewing maybe, not much else.
SHANNON	Did you know, I was going to be a wood engraver before I met him.
HETTY	And now you're a painter. Do you think there's much difference?

> *SHANNON goes to her to fix the apple. She grabs him into a kiss.*

SHANNON	I do.
HETTY	Where is he?
SHANNON	Picking up our Tanagra.
HETTY	What's a Tanagra?
SHANNON	An ancient Greek terracotta figurine. Very charming.
HETTY	Very expensive?
SHANNON	Our banking account will vanish.
HETTY	Really.
SHANNON	We put the deposit down months ago.
HETTY	*(swatting SHANNON playfully)* I knew I should have resisted you.
SHANNON	But you couldn't. I mean I'm glad you didn't. You were my first, you know.
HETTY	That was abundantly clear.

SHANNON	I needed to know first if I liked it.
HETTY	(*resisting him, playfully*) If you insist on spending foolishly, it's only fair to alert you, I am considering other offers.
SHANNON	Hedging your bets, are you?
HETTY	Captain Robert Falcon Scott has been most persistent.
SHANNON	I'm sure his snot-frosted mustaches and blackened toes would charm any bride.
HETTY	He's going to claim the earth's farthest reaches for all of England.
SHANNON	Well I'd rather claim you.
HETTY	Well? Then tell the apple-man.
SHANNON	I did. Yesterday, after Lincolnshire.

> *Split stage, different times. RICKETTS scurries into the drawing room. He hangs a sizable square framed drawing prominently on the wall.*

HETTY	What did he say?
SHANNON	It's not as simple as that.
HETTY	It's very simple. You are leaving him.
SHANNON	I told him, Hetty. But as usual, Ricketts had his own surprise.

— • —

> *RICKETTS puts finishing touches on his display. HETTY watches on as if being told the story.*

RICKETTS	How was the train?
SHANNON	(*calling over*) Fine. Mother and Father send their regards.

RICKETTS   You covered in cow dung?

SHANNON   Reek of it, I'm sure. Where are you?

RICKETTS   Drawing room!

> *SHANNON "enters" RICKETTS's area. He does not yet notice the painting.*

SHANNON   Ricketts.

RICKETTS   Chubbers. Lovely to see your red face again.

SHANNON   Oh, uh... from the wind, I'm sure.

RICKETTS   (*squirming in distracted, delicious anticipation*) Teasing!

SHANNON   I need to wash. Would you pour me a sherry?

RICKETTS   Stay. Sit. Look around. What's wrong?

SHANNON   Well, Ricketts, I suppose a dissatisfaction with the *status quo*. We're known as "bachelor companions." As such we must recognise that bachelors often fulfill their natural... (*Turning, he finally sees the painting. Overwhelmed, he forgets himself.*) Puvis de Chavannes?

RICKETTS   Yes! A sanguine study, the last in private hands.

SHANNON   Ricketts, how much did it–

RICKETTS   Only a hundred and thirty-four pounds.

SHANNON   Oh Lord, we're broke.

RICKETTS   You should have seen me. E.J. had called me in to look at this Persian tracing. Magnificent, but a bit stiff at forty pounds.

SHANNON   I should say!

RICKETTS And then I turned around, not unlike you did just here. I burst into a sweat at the sight of it.

SHANNON So it's... it's ours?

RICKETTS It's as if we have a ballast now from all the ugliness of the past months. These two labourers working together, a perfect specimen of composition, line, musculature...

SHANNON (*shift*) Yes. Ricketts...

RICKETTS You remember that day at the Louvre those years ago, how the artist himself infused our dreams with direction? You remember that night?

SHANNON It's just a drawing...

RICKETTS "Just" a...? Shannon!

SHANNON I'm afraid your timing is off.

RICKETTS (*stop, looking close at him*) Oh Lord – your mother. Is she–

SHANNON She's fine. I went with Hetty.

RICKETTS To Lincolnshire? Overnight? Why?

SHANNON Because I'm fond of her.

RICKETTS No reason to have her crowding up a train compartment.

SHANNON I wanted her to meet my family.

RICKETTS (*pause*) Oh?

SHANNON Ricketts. Don't make me spell it out.

RICKETTS I rather think you'd better.

SHANNON Hetty and I, we–

RICKETTS   No. No. No. You are not going to say this. This is
another of your ridiculous reactions to that, that
brouhaha with Oscar.

SHANNON   I'm in love with her, Charles.

RICKETTS   She's a, a, a painter's model! Jabbering on about
her quest for good heroic stock, and what, *you're*
her sire?

SHANNON   I know my heart. I love her.

RICKETTS   I'm afraid your heart sits rather lower than it once
did.

SHANNON   Just what are you implying?

RICKETTS   The lump you claim you feel in your throat is
really in your trousers.

SHANNON   You bastard.

RICKETTS   Go ruin your paintings with her face if you like.
Immortalise her. Rut her regularly her if you
must. But my God, what can she give you?
Conversation? Criticism?

SHANNON   Children.

RICKETTS   (*beat*) You... you are a great painter. You don't
need–

SHANNON   I'm not a great painter. When are you going to
realise that?

RICKETTS   Shannon...

SHANNON   I am thirty-three years old.

RICKETTS   And what, you're in search of a crucifixion?

SHANNON   I will never be "the master." Our great plan never
worked.

RICKETTS   You've had exhibitions, portrait commissions. Your paintings sell.

SHANNON   But every day is such a struggle. Every painting, every brush-stroke is wrung out of me. And for what? Who out there cares if I paint?

RICKETTS   I do. Fifteen years I've supported you.

SHANNON   And where am I?

RICKETTS   On the cusp of greatness.

SHANNON   You're the only one who says so.

RICKETTS   The rest of them are idiots! You think Delacroix was appreciated in his lifetime?

SHANNON   Yes.

RICKETTS   Fair enough, bad example. So, so Hetty gets her hands on you and then what: You'll teach at some art school, make enough to keep a squalid house full of children. Is that what you want? Our time has been fragile, but that is no reason to despise a thing. Fashions will change–

SHANNON   Yes, and when they do, we'll be left even further behind.

RICKETTS   She bit you. You're poisoned.

SHANNON   What if we're not the future of anything? What if we're the last gasp – before it all expires into a cold heap of irrelevance? I can't go the rest of my life like this. I want something to live after me.

SHANNON goes to leave. RICKETTS stops him.

RICKETTS   Our collection. The Greek pots, Sheffield jugs, Verrochio's "Cupid and Dolphin." Rossetti's "Mary Magdalen," Watteau's flute player, the Perugino – damaged, yes, but genuine. The Utamaro prints, Lorraine's drawings. Our Rubens, our Millet. Think of them.

(HETTY   (*in the other "world"*) Just let him have them.)

SHANNON   I can't.

RICKETTS   What if you're wrong? What if you give up now, just before the grace of genius is fulfilled in you? Will you ever forgive yourself?

SHANNON   I'll never know, will I.

RICKETTS   You will. In your soul you'll know.

> *Faced with this challenge, SHANNON starts to leave. RICKETTS calls after him.*

The Tanagra arrives tomorrow.

(HETTY   Can't you just leave it?)

SHANNON   No.

RICKETTS   Yes, our beloved Tanagra we've waited these months for. What am I supposed to do?

— • —

> *SHANNON returns to HETTY, now on the bed with her, high energy.*

HETTY   Then take your half; I could live with them.

SHANNON   I couldn't. I'd shatter something whole. The pieces would be like grieving orphans.

HETTY   There are more important things in life than, well, than *things*.

SHANNON   Can you feel how perfect it is in this house? The inexhaustible genius on the walls: Oily Italian flourishes are tempered by austere Japanese prints. Quiet Dutch landscapes cool the torrid mythic paintings. What could I take from here?

HETTY	Take me. I am flesh. I'm not paint. See my body? Feel it – no, feel it. This is not stretched canvas – it's skin, warm skin, with blood and a beating heart underneath. Why is that so terrifying to you?

An offstage door slams. Pause.

SHANNON	He's back with the Tanagra.
HETTY	A bloody lump of clay.
SHANNON	He has nobody else, you know. No family.
HETTY	Oh, and is that your fault?
SHANNON	What if he's right about me? What if I'm teetering on the edge, only too afraid to open my eyes and see it? I've caught glimpses, Hetty, of what the world still needs. What will endure and not just add to the clutter. What if I'm on the verge of letting it pour out of me?

Elsewhere, RICKETTS enters an area with a packing box. He gingerly unpacks the Tanagra.

(RICKETTS	(*to the Tanagra*) Welcome home, you...)

Upset, HETTY starts to leave the bed and get dressed.

SHANNON	Hetty. I'm painting you. I'm paying you to be here.
HETTY	Then we're both breaking promises, aren't we.
(RICKETTS	(*sponging the Tanagra in a basin*) Let's clean you up here, you little rapscallion...)
SHANNON	This is a... difficult extrication. He's the only one who believes in me.
HETTY	I believe in you too; I believe you could be a husband, a father, and yes, a painter. A good one.

But you'll never be his Michelangelo. And that means, in his eyes, you'll always be a failure.

As RICKETTS washes the Tanagra, the face begins to crumble. He panics, tears welling.

(RICKETTS   Oh God.)

HETTY   I'm not just a painter's model. I'm a women with a vision of a splendid life. So ask yourself whose dream you're more likely to fulfill: his or mine?

(RICKETTS   No! Shannon?)

SHANNON   (*hearing*) Something's wrong.

HETTY   Don't go.

(RICKETTS   Shannon!)

SHANNON   He knows I'm in here.

HETTY   I'll not wait forever.

SHANNON   Time. I just need some time.

SHANNON goes to RICKETTS and finds him wretched.

RICKETTS   I was cleaning it and... the face split where it was mended here and...

SHANNON   It's all here.

RICKETTS   A piece fell into the basin. My heart leapt into my mouth and then dived out after it.

SHANNON   We'll mend it again. Just a little moist clay is all you need. It's all right.

RICKETTS   What would I do? I'm nothing. Chubbs, what would I do?

> *SHANNON holds the distraught RICKETTS.*
> *Slowly, he is calmed.*
>
> *Elsewhere, HETTY finishes dressing. Taking a bite*
> *of an apple, she leaves.*

SHANNON   I paint perfect worlds. Each canvas is a carefully crafted view, mythic figures rendered as real as the flesh of a lover. I play God. And face the creator's question: when to stop. It's so easy, fueled by the elation of making something of nothing, to get proud, to go too far and add one brushstroke I shouldn't. Once committed, of course, that choice can't ever be reversed. I can only try to fix my mistake with more brushstrokes, adding more and more paint, stupidly covering perfection as I try to accommodate what was utterly wrong to begin with. That one small slip had changed everything. I don't know anything worse than the sadness I feel when I've taken what was once nearly perfect, and sent it... sent it to ruin.

5.

> *SHANNON finds a journal and opens it. The*
> *space transforms into a barren waiting room, two*
> *simple chairs and a table, no art. RICKETTS*
> *sits, nervous and cold, perhaps having not moved,*
> *only objects around him having moved. Thomas*
> *MARTIN the prison warder enters.*

MARTIN   You the one waiting for him?

RICKETTS   I am.

(SHANNON   I learned this from his journals.)

MARTIN   Sorry it's so frigging cold.

(SHANNON   He left them for me.)

RICKETTS   I'm sure it keeps the mind nimble.

(SHANNON	Hoping I'd know where to look.)
MARTIN	You know his books and all that?
RICKETTS	Actually, I published all his books. Illustrated them too.
MARTIN	Hm. I thought there was that skinny bloke who–
RICKETTS	(*sharp*) Except one. All except one.
MARTIN	Hm. Seen his plays?
RICKETTS	Oh yes.
MARTIN	My mate Tupper, he saw Lady Windermere with Miss Ellen Terry in it. Says it was splendid. I wish I had been there. Wish I had half his brains. His, not Tupper's.
RICKETTS	How is he?
MARTIN	Off the plank now so maybe he'll start sleeping. Won't choke down much of his suet and skilly so he's shrinking. The diarrhoea doesn't help. Fills his tin all night till his slops cover the floor. I'm sick with disgust to open his cell in the morning. Wretched what comes out of a man.
RICKETTS	There are days one regrets one is an Englishman.
MARTIN	I wouldn't go *that* far...
RICKETTS	To think, I sat waiting for him the night he was arrested.

OSCAR Wilde enters, wan and shrunken, perhaps escorted. MARTIN stands.

OSCAR	As I've said, it is always nice to be expected and not to arrive.
RICKETTS	Oscar.

MARTIN	I'll leave you.
OSCAR	Very kind.
	MARTIN exits.
	Welcome to my parlour.
RICKETTS	Oscar. Your hands, they're cracked and shredded.
OSCAR	I can't bear your tears, man. Think where you are.
RICKETTS	Yes. Shannon sends his regards.
OSCAR	Tell him I often think of his handsome face. What do you want.
RICKETTS	Advice.
OSCAR	There's no wisdom in these walls.
RICKETTS	Oh? I imagine you brimming with ideas. A new play? *Lady Windermere's Fan* has recently been given in Richmond.
OSCAR	Yes, banished to Richmond.
RICKETTS	The warder was telling me his friend quite liked it.
OSCAR	Ah Martin. Advice you say. No doubt regarding the National Gallery. I hear you've been offered the dictatorship.
RICKETTS	Oh, that? No, I shan't accept, of course.
OSCAR	Why ever not?
RICKETTS	Would *you* be a glorified civil servant? No. You live for beauty.
OSCAR	Yes, and closed my eyes while it kissed me in the garden.

RICKETTS   Don't despair – we'll hold you a big party when you get out.

OSCAR   What for.

RICKETTS   Conversation, that most ephemeral of arts. We thought it a handsome way to welcome you back into society.

OSCAR   Everyone's obsessed with my post-prison itinerary. "Friends" natter about Venice.

RICKETTS   A worthy destination.

OSCAR   To sink in fetid silence? No, I shall move to Dieppe.

RICKETTS   But Oscar, Dieppe is so... beneath you!

OSCAR   I shall find it within my means and very agreeable.

RICKETTS   It is filled with the English. They will only stare at you.

OSCAR   Then I shall stare back. I wish to look at life, Ricketts. I am not so inclined to cultivate the rarefied distance you swear by. That in itself is a kind of prison.

RICKETTS   (*beat, handing him a small basket of apples*) This will cheer you. It's small, but...

OSCAR   Very kind. I shall give it to Martin.

RICKETTS   The warder? He can have an apple any time he likes!

OSCAR   Ah, but he doesn't.

RICKETTS   He is your captor.

OSCAR   He is my friend. I confess I find fruit unpalatable. Tastes of sunshine and wind. Apollo and Zephyrus wither in this place. They both loved that boy Hyacinthus, poor fools.

RICKETTS   You allude to Bosie.

OSCAR   Your purpose, Ricketts. I am tired.

RICKETTS   Oscar, how did you make him love you?

OSCAR   Wine, poetry and narcotics.

RICKETTS   Come now. Bosie is still devoted to you. He still defends your name.

OSCAR   Anything to keep his in the papers. His beauty allows him to behave in ugly ways.

RICKETTS   That's not always the case.

OSCAR   Of course it is. Beauty demands the soul's sacrifice – you've read *Dorian Gray*.

RICKETTS   And you know Shannon. He is both beautiful and good. And Oscar, I'm afraid he'll leave me. I thought of you and Bosie and I wondered...

OSCAR   How ugly old Oscar could beguile such a fair young man?

RICKETTS   Well, yes. Shannon's convinced he's in love with one of his models.

OSCAR   Is this infatuation or is it a serious affair–

RICKETTS   I don't know! I've been too busy ignoring it. He's my only family; no one else can bear me.

OSCAR   Do you love him? (*beat*) It's difficult to answer, isn't it, when asked so baldly by an angry interrogator.

RICKETTS   I do love him, in a way. In the best way.

OSCAR	Then consider what sacrifice you are prepared to make.
RICKETTS	Why should *I* make a sacrifice?
OSCAR	Bosie knew what I gave up to defend our love.
RICKETTS	And what did you get in return?
OSCAR	Had I thought about myself, Ricketts, I wouldn't be here. You must be prepared to let everything go. Faced with such an awesome and touching surrender, he will make a clean choice.
RICKETTS	But I have to stop him. If he left I'd have nothing.
OSCAR	Did you know, cold is worse than hunger. I should not have guessed this to be the case. But in time one can get used to the latter. The warders bring me treats: meat pies and sausage rolls. I surprise myself each time I choke one down. Astonishing, the capacities of a hungry man.

And with that, OSCAR turns and leaves.

6.

SHANNON pulls a letter from the journal and reads it, posing as RICKETTS paints him. They stay in place as the world around them turns back to their drawing room.

SHANNON	(*reading RICKETTS's letter*) So you'll accept. Ricketts, you won't regret this.
RICKETTS	Of course I will: the job will shorten my life.
SHANNON	It will make it bearable. You'll finally have money, prestige...
RICKETTS	...A bureaucrat's sagging bottom...

SHANNON   (*teasing*) You've dithered so long now, they've probably gone and hired Roger Fry.

RICKETTS   Fry? As director? That little ferret is blind to beauty. He'd fill galleries with that Impressionist bilge the Continent calls art.

SHANNON   Then you'll save the National Gallery from his bad taste.

RICKETTS   Sit still, Chubbers, or I'll ruin your nose.

SHANNON   To spite my sunny face?

RICKETTS   Yes, I'll prick it with hundreds of *pointillist* dots!

SHANNON   Oo! Ow! Stop or I'll expose your traitorous taste to the trustees! Your brushes are behaving so badly I shall have to buy you new ones.

RICKETTS   Extravagance!

SHANNON   You're the new arbiter of taste in this country, enjoy it.

RICKETTS   Yes. (*beat*) I was thinking Venice in spring.

SHANNON   Can we afford it?

RICKETTS   As Director of the National Gallery I can. We could bask on the Lido's sand, bake ourselves red, warm up again. Say yes. It's the best I can do.

> *Just then, BEARDSLEY appears in the doorway. Breathless, sickly and even paler than before, he wears the same Eton jacket. Now wrinkled and worn, it hangs from his frame.*

BEARDSLEY   Hello.

RICKETTS   Oh! Good God. Beardsley.

SHANNON   What a surprise.

BEARDSLEY   The door was open.

SHANNON   Come in.

RICKETTS   You look like one of your wretched drawings.

SHANNON   We were just celebrating.

RICKETTS   I am to accept the directorship of the National Gallery.

BEARDSLEY   (*toasting from a bottle of medicine*) Your health and happiness. (*by way of explanation*) Doctor Harsant's Hæmorrhage Mix

RICKETTS   They've been courting me for months as you've no doubt heard. Have you come seeking a spot on the walls?

SHANNON   Ricketts...

RICKETTS   Your purpose, Beardsley. We have guests arriving.

BEARDSLEY   Heard you saw Oscar.

RICKETTS   He's fit as a fiddle. Be in top form when he gets out.

BEARDSLEY   I really must arrange a visit before I leave town.

RICKETTS   Why? He knows the appalling things you've been saying about him.

BEARDSLEY   Well? I am broke and he's to blame. Writers refuse to publish with anyone who employs "Daubaway Weirdsley." Oscar's the burnished barge that carried me and others so far. It has sprung a leak and the resulting geyser has soaked those who rode it.

SHANNON   And so you come for assistance from the equally drenched.

BEARDSLEY   Yes. Say. Is that a Tanagra? Is it real?

RICKETTS   I can recognise a fake when I see one.

SHANNON   Why are you leaving London?

BEARDSLEY   (*coughing*) I must... go... to... France.

SHANNON   Nobody will prosecute you now, old boy.

> *BEARDSLEY's body is wracked with coughs.*
> *RICKETTS shrinks back in disgust. SHANNON*
> *hovers over him, nervously trying to catch the*
> *Tanagra should it fall. He extricates it and sets it*
> *down. BEARDSLEY coughs a long while, his old*
> *handkerchief stained with blood and mucous.*

BEARDSLEY   I know. This may surprise you but I'm not one of
the wilting pansies who've fled the country or cut
their hair and loudly subscribed to the Times
Cricket Fund. I'm associated with a criminal vice
which, while it amuses my imagination, has never
dictated my actions.

SHANNON   You like women.

BEARDSLEY   Yes. That has been *my* secret.

SHANNON   I understand, Aubrey.

BEARDSLEY   My name, you know, means ruler of the fairies.
But not myself a fairy. Instead, a blemished
gargoyle. I flee to France for the air. I trust
you'll help a dying man.

RICKETTS   You've got nerve.

BEARDSLEY   Do not mistake desperation for courage.

RICKETTS   You have squandered all your money? God, if I'd
only had your life.

BEARDSLEY   You wouldn't have wanted it.

RICKETTS   I wouldn't have *wasted* it.

BEARDSLEY	You'd have clutched life so close, any wealth or inspiration would have suffocated.
SHANNON	Ricketts is an exceedingly generous man.
BEARDSLEY	Yes. So I'd heard.
RICKETTS	You have lost your charms. Look at you, come so boldly begging...
BEARDSLEY	What, you want the old game again? I'm tired of the dandy's mask. I wore it because I was a frightened boy thrust into an arena with ruthless lions who sought to devour me for my luck, my talent, the sheen of my success. I'd never have survived without a veil to hide behind. But now what use have I for charm or wit or fear of men when I am coughing myself to death?
SHANNON	(*pause*) How much do you need?
BEARDSLEY	Whatever you can spare.
RICKETTS	We can't–
SHANNON	We can. With your new job, it's the least we can do.
	HOLMES enters, having bounded upstairs, breathless.
RICKETTS	Ah yes. Youth and beauty. Come in and save us.
HOLMES	I have news. You'll be so pleased.
BEARDSLEY	News. Of course. Every day there is news.
RICKETTS	You're looking well, you beastly rotter. New suit?
HOLMES	Yes. Beardsley, hello. Why don't you sit down?
SHANNON	Ricketts has decided to accept the offer of the directorship of the National Gallery.

RICKETTS   *I* wanted to tell him!

HOLMES   Charles...

RICKETTS   I've been coy these past weeks.

SHANNON   Feared the job would shorten his life.

RICKETTS   It will.

SHANNON   Still, it's the greatest opportunity he'll ever be offered, don't you think?

HOLMES   I hope not.

RICKETTS   My delay will only make them ravenous to have me.

HOLMES   Oh dear...

RICKETTS   I'll likely be offered twice the salary–

HOLMES   Ricketts. The job has actually been offered to someone else. Just today.

BEARDSLEY   Well!

RICKETTS   Fry?

HOLMES   No.

**RICKETTS &
BEARDSLEY**   Thank God.

SHANNON   Who?

HOLMES   (*beat*) Me.

RICKETTS   You? The uh, the directorship of the National Gallery?

HOLMES   Yes.

BEARDSLEY   (*pause*) Congratulations.

RICKETTS   Yes, yes! Congratulations.

HOLMES   If I'd known you were still interested...

RICKETTS   Not at all. We've launched you into glory. Wonderful, isn't it, Shannon.

SHANNON   Impressive, what a little initiative will get you.

KATHERINE & EDITH   (*calling from off*) Hallooooo!

SHANNON   Our guests have arrived.

RICKETTS   Mister Beardsley...?

HOLMES   I should go too.

SHANNON   No. Please stay.

BEARDSLEY   I wonder if I might as well.

RICKETTS   What kind of bloody farce is this?

> *Pause. KATHERINE and EDITH then sweep in, each reading from identical slim volumes. As they banter, the four men stand glum and stunned.*

KATHERINE   "Forth, forth, away! He is not of these halls, / No motion of him there, Whym Chow no sound: / His ruby head shall never strike these walls, / And nowhere by a cry shall he be found."

EDITH   "O little Dog, O little Chow! / What beating of fine, little feet! / What slouch of ears like banners droop!"

SHANNON   Your new book.

KATHERINE   Has arrived!

HOLMES   Congratulations.

BEARDSLEY   What's the subject.

EDITH   Death.

RICKETTS   (*dropping brushes*) Good Lord.

KATHERINE   Inspired by a spiritual crisis arising out of our grief over the demise of our much-loved dog.

BEARDSLEY   Its title?

EDITH   *Whym Chow: Flame of Love.*

BEARDSLEY   A passionate epitaph.

KATHERINE   We were very attached to him.

**EDITH &
KATHERINE**   "Loud Halls, O Hades of the living! On! / What, are the swarming little cries not heard? / What, are the lit bright feet for ever gone / Or yet to swifter orbit were they spurred?"

KATHERINE   We expect the book to sell out its entire print run.

HOLMES   Ambitious.

BEARDSLEY   Enviable. How many were printed?

**KATHERINE
& EDITH**   Twenty-Seven!

HOLMES   Books.

KATHERINE   Yes. An exclusive audience.

BEARDSLEY   A nonexistent one...

KATHERINE   Our publisher has complained of losses.

EDITH   The Twentieth Century infests taste like scorpions or lice or all things of creeping filth and slime!

> *BEARDSLEY takes a draught of medicine. Pause.*

KATHERINE   Fay, you are painting!

RICKETTS   Yes, Michael, that's what we do here.

KATHERINE   And what has the muse summoned...

RICKETTS   Get away.

EDITH   It was only to offer encouragement.

RICKETTS   And do you think I want the opinion of such frivolous anachronisms as you? Really: an ode to a dead dog is laughable. A whole book of them verges on madness.

KATHERINE   Then you shan't receive a copy, you beastly man. Luckily there are others who appreciate our heart's labours. Isn't that right, gentlemen? (*Silence. She takes offence.*) Well.

EDITH   We put our hearts into these poems.

RICKETTS   ...Stifling exhalations of sentimentality.

KATHERINE   What do you know of love and loss?

RICKETTS   I know loss.

EDITH   Then why laugh at ours?

RICKETTS   It's not real.

EDITH   It *is* real to us, in our souls.

RICKETTS   Then your souls are shrunken. They are not the souls of artists.

BEARDSLEY   Nobody reads your books now.

EDITH   We enjoy writing them.

BEARDSLEY   What are you known for besides sharing the same bed, aunt and niece?

RICKETTS	What have you done that has made a jig of difference?
KATHERINE	We are happy! The vagaries of fashion and cruel happenstance cannot tarnish our joy. Which of you men can claim that?
HOLMES	(*pause*) I... I am happy.
EDITH	Come, Michael.
KATHERINE	Is that it? Nothing else to say? Ah, for once, silence. What we have "done," gentlemen, is write our plays and poems with joy. Would our books have been more successful if we'd suffered writing them? We think not. While you men lash yourselves with regret and self-loathing, we have found love, in our friendships, in our home – and yes, Mister Beardsley, in our bed. We like to think those are the measures of a good life.
BEARDSLEY	Mrs.... Field. I'd like to purchase a book, for my trip.
EDITH	We shall forgive, Mister Beardsley.
KATHERINE	But not forget.
EDITH	Accept a copy as our gift.
KATHERINE	So many gifts you men possess. Neither joy nor peace among them.

KATHERINE and EDITH exit.

BEARDSLEY	I'll read it. Goodness knows, with my hatchet face, I'll never have a love to grieve.
SHANNON	(*writing a cheque*) Thank you for coming by, Holmes. It's a great honour for you.
RICKETTS	Yes, I'd have thought Fry would get the job. I suppose he didn't want it either.

HOLMES	I suppose.
SHANNON	May you find a good woman in France, Mister Beardsley.
BEARDSLEY	Can you manage so much...
RICKETTS	No. So you'd better leave before I change his mind.
HOLMES	I'll take you home.
BEARDSLEY	An ambush of kindness in the twilight.

HOLMES leads BEARDSLEY off. RICKETTS and SHANNON are alone.

RICKETTS	I rather hate my friends.
SHANNON	There's a fearful symmetry to that.
RICKETTS	Holmes has wilfully usurped me.
SHANNON	He has succeeded, nothing more. I'm sure you're relieved: if you couldn't groan under the weight of an indifferent world, you'd dry up and blow away.
RICKETTS	You should leave me. (*pause*) For Hetty.
SHANNON	You don't mean that.
RICKETTS	I do. I'm making a sacrifice now, a proper sacrifice.
SHANNON	Your "sacrifices" are the writhings of a fool grasping at tragedy.
RICKETTS	You can always come back tomorrow. But tonight, you have a woman who loves you. Think how happy you would make her. Go.
SHANNON	I have a good mind to.
RICKETTS	Good. Then leave. Leave me!

SHANNON   I will.

RICKETTS   Shannon, wait. One thing. Take your painting of me.

SHANNON   I'm not trudging around London with a painting under my–

RICKETTS   Do and you may leave without guilt. But that canvas needs to be with you, a reminder.

SHANNON   What, of you?

RICKETTS   Of *our* capacities. Of the genius that's in you.

SHANNON   What if I want to forget that.

RICKETTS   Then you really are a coward.

> *Pause. SHANNON gets the ladder. RICKETTS wistfully admires the painting.*

I like the pose. There I am, turning utterly away from the Twentieth Century. Turning, yes, turning to think only of the Fifteenth.

> *RICKETTS turns and leaves the room. Ladder in place, SHANNON climbs it.*

SHANNON   And so he turned and left the room. I climbed the ladder. Why? Did I jump or was I pushed? The painting was mine, an early work after our first trip to Paris. It's of a man I loved and yet could not love. I reached for that beautiful canvas. Reached dangerously back to the sweet early days. I reached too far.

> *He reaches off the ladder. Grabbing the painting, he falls and lands unconscious on the floor. The fall can be either startlingly real or suggestive through a slow-motion stylisation. SHANNON lands motionless on the floor, the painting crashing down beside him. Silence.*

RICKETTS   (*offstage*) Shannon? (*pause*) Shannon! Where are you?

> *RICKETTS enters holding a porcelain bowl filled with apples. He drops it when he sees SHANNON. It breaks, the apples rolling everywhere. Otherwise, stillness.*

Charles.

> *Blackout.*

> *Intermission.*

l to r: Vickie Papavs, Julian Ritchings, Oliver Dennis
photo by Nir Bareket

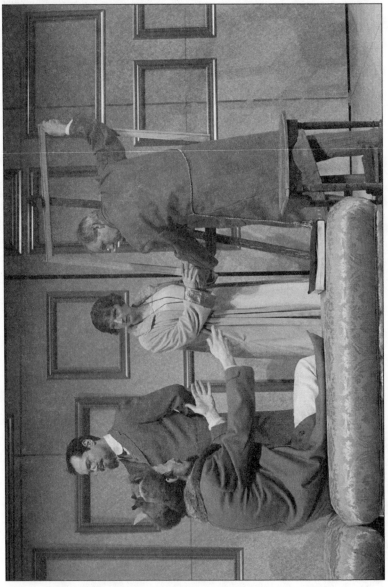

l to r: Julian Ritchings, Jonathan Crombie, Kate Hennig, Oliver Dennis
photo by Nir Bareket

l to r: Julian Ritchings, Oliver Dennis
photo by Nir Bareket

—•— Act Two —•—

7.

A small light reveals a brush on the floor.
SHANNON appears, a shadow in darkness.
He approaches the pool of light and looks down
at the brush, then peers out to the audience.

SHANNON   Time has passed, drawing us years closer to you. You've missed a lot, though nothing as spectacular as my skull's vanquishing. It was an overly dramatic flourish, but I had to be sure you'd return.

He reaches tentatively, then picks up the brush.
Lights fill the drawing room revealing EDITH
with the clipboard, older as at the beginning.
Ignoring him, she busies herself itemizing the
remaining art. She leaves before the scene's end.

Our home here was crowded with beauty. It thickened the walls, a fortress against the world's obvious progression. They're taking it away now, in front of my eyes. Because I fell.

He begins to paint in the air.

Bang, it was sudden – the way inspiration arrives. I smashed the front of my brain, the part that elevates us from lesser animals. It's nothing more than a spongy, pitted plum in the skull's bowl, but in the lucky, it produces genius. Mine had been dashed to the ground. I stood among the pieces, dead and curiously still living. I tried to retrieve myself, bits of the past I gathered and dropped, gathered and dropped like a greedy child harvesting fruit.

SHANNON paints a huge, sloppy circle in the air.
Above him, rendered through light, a huge sun
appears illuminating everything.

RICKETTS   (*offstage*) Sun!

SHANNON   My life was a stammering tantrum.

RICKETTS   (*entering*) The sun!

SHANNON   I'd given up.

8.

*Park, setting sun, sound of birds and distant
machinery. Each with a sketchpad, SHANNON
and RICKETTS draw, SHANNON aimlessly,
brain-damaged by the fall. Others promenade past.*

RICKETTS   Sun! The sun! Isn't it glorious?

SHANNON   Sunnnn...

RICKETTS   You're not even looking at it. (*grabbing his face*)
Come now. Sun. See? Sun.

SHANNON   (*squinting*) Uhhhnn!

RICKETTS   Speak properly. (*suffering slight angina*) Christ,
you're killing me.

SHANNON   (*pause*) Sun.

RICKETTS   Sun, yes. Remember how hard it was to paint
Apollo's orb?

SHANNON   How hard.

RICKETTS   Good! Well, when we look at the sun it's only a
glance, a bright, flaming miracle we barely grasp.
But the eye can lazily linger on a canvas for hours.
So a painted sun must have such indelible power
that one glance sears the mind forever. Only one
painting ever did that, remember?

SHANNON   Fifty-five fifty-five fifty-five, hear sixty, sixty...

RICKETTS   Of course you remember; it changed your life.
The Piero di Cosimo.

> *A passing cloaked man (PUVIS) reveals himself to*
> *SHANNON. RICKETTS doesn't notice.*

PUVIS   *Charmante! Charmante jeunesse!*

SHANNON   *Charmante...*

RICKETTS   Yes! In Paris. Puvis owned it. Everything started when you set eyes on that painting. And now it's up for sale. The Bensons...

SHANNON   Sun!

RICKETTS   ...are liquidating their collection.

SHANNON   Sixty, sixty / sixty, hear sixty-five, sixty-five...

RICKETTS   The poor fools have trifled away their wealth – still, their loss is our gain. We can't afford it of course, but I have a plan. You'll set eyes on it again. Then you'll see.

SHANNON   Buhhhnnn...

RICKETTS   An expressive use of line there, Chubbs, I can see Giotto's influence. Though we must work on your mastery of perspective, depth on a flat surface.

SHANNON   Aaaaaaaarrrrrrrrhhhh.

RICKETTS   Well keep trying. An artist must work despite adversity. What are you drawing?

SHANNON   Her.

RICKETTS   Who? There's no – oh Lord. Come on, Chubbs.

SHANNON   Her! Her!

HETTY   (*entering wheeling a pram*) Mister Ricketts?

RICKETTS   Miss Bruce! What a surprise.

SHANNON   Hah! Hahhhhhhh!

RICKETTS	Lovely day, isn't it.
HETTY	Oh. Charles. Hello.
RICKETTS	It's been decades, Miss Bruce. He won't know you.
SHANNON	Nnnnnnnn...
HETTY	Look at you, still the same.
RICKETTS	Yes, Shannon found the fountain of youth, unscathed by the Twentieth Century.
SHANNON	Hetty...
RICKETTS	Good God.
HETTY	He does know me. Charles.
RICKETTS	He doesn't know anyone except me. He merely fancies he does.
HETTY	He seems quite lucid.
RICKETTS	My pursuit of his recovery has consumed me, Miss Bruce. You don't just waltz past and catalyse an apotheosis.
HETTY	I'll thank you to address me as Lady Scott.
RICKETTS	I don't concern myself with titles and other trivialities. (*baby*) Coo coo coo.
HETTY	Nothing trivial about Captain Robert Scott.
SHANNON	Coo coo coo!
HETTY	Every child in England learns about him. He will certainly be remembered.
RICKETTS	For tramping about our polar extremes? Rather an outdated occupation, explorer.

HETTY	Not at all: for those brave enough there are always uncharted places, territories without claim. My husband tested the limits of endurance and courage. His rough notes and dead body bore a message to stir the heart of every brave man that might follow him. He died a hero's death and left a great legacy: two sons.
RICKETTS	And now a grandmother?
HETTY	Fertile stock, Mr. Ricketts.
SHANNON	(*investigating HETTY*) Mmmm. Lllllllady.
HETTY	Charles. Hello.
RICKETTS	I made my own New World foray. I run Canada's National Gallery. Practically.
HETTY	I can't imagine you making the trip.
RICKETTS	Good God, I haven't actually gone over. I buy paintings for them and ship them off. I admit I can use the commission. We have the king's doctor and a team of nurses looking after him. But more important, I am shaping a nation's culture.

> *He rattles on unaware that SHANNON has begun to hump HETTY's hip. She tries to dodge him, mute from mortification and propriety. RICKETTS continues, oblivious.*

	They have so little of it over there, you know. So little past. They are rather like Mr. Shannon here in their need for memory. Why not visit us, see our collection. You do seem to... help him. Shannon might benefit from the social intercour– Charles!
SHANNON	Fffffffffffffff! Fuh! Fuh! Fuh!
RICKETTS	Charles! No! (*pulling him away*) Good Lord, Miss uh... I'm–

HETTY	Charles... Charles, it's me!
SHANNON	(*struck by RICKETTS*) Aaaaahhhhh!
HETTY	Stop it!
RICKETTS	You don't... you don't know...
HETTY	Oh I do, very well. You did this.
RICKETTS	It was an accident, Miss Bruce. He fell.
SHANNON	Fifty fifty, / hear forty-five, forty five, forty-five...
HETTY	But you pushed. I hope you can forgive yourself for destroying him, because I certainly can't.
RICKETTS	Destroy? I made him! (*angina*)
SHANNON	Fffaaaaaaahhhhhhh!
HETTY	Yes, into exactly what you wanted.
SHANNON	I... I...!
RICKETTS	The best he could be.
HETTY	What's that? Someone incapable of leaving you?
SHANNON	Wait! I! I!
HETTY	There was a time, Charles, I know. But it's better now if you forget. Goodbye.
SHANNON	Lost? No! You. You b-broke me. She was m-mine! Mine!
	As HETTY wheels off the pram, SHANNON crumples. RICKETTS comforts him, unmoved.
RICKETTS	Yes, she was yours. That, you remember. That. Depth on a flat surface. You're still in the picture. See Titian's ripe clouds? See the smudge of a Turner horizon? And there's Piero's sun, the

most astonishing sun ever painted. Remember that sun?

SHANNON   Nnnnnnnn.

RICKETTS   Just look up and you'll see it. Just look. Please. See? Can you see beauty there?

SHANNON   No.

RICKETTS   You will. When you see that painting again, you will.

SHANNON   (*to audience*) When I saw her again, I did. See beauty. After so many years, the lizard-skin was seared from my eyes. It was a vague memory, muddy like a bad oil painting. But it was something to aim for. I took up my brush again, hoping I might dream the past to life.

9.

Split scene. BROWN and RICKETTS look at paintings at an auction gallery. Elsewhere SHANNON sets a canvas on an easel. He hallucinates an imaginary world.

RICKETTS   Imagine this painting, Brown: an exquisite Piero di Cosimo once owned by the great nineteenth century painter, Puvis de Chavannes. I think we should buy it.

BROWN   You know where I can buy some uh Lovely Lydia Lavender Soap?

RICKETTS   Soap.

BROWN   My wife bought a bar here in London on our honeymoon. You Brits may not appreciate the finer points of plumbing, but you sure know your soap.

RICKETTS	And we certainly don't want your new bride scaling up.
BROWN	You don't know Ottawa winters. We keep buckets of water in the gallery just to stop paint from flaking off the canvasses.
RICKETTS	Brown, as director of your National Gallery, you must assure the art's preservation.
BROWN	The paintings lasted wars and plagues, I doubt a mere colony could ruin them. Here.
RICKETTS	Picasso? Oh, Brown...
BROWN	Well, it is European art.
RICKETTS	Only the desperate resort to geography.
BROWN	I'm not asking you to like it–
RICKETTS	You're new to your job, Mr. Brown. Please remember, I advise your trustees directly. They expect an honest assessment.
BROWN	Compared to your Old Masters this is a bargain.
RICKETTS	Thusly compared, Brown, it's worthless. Show me the other one.

— • —

SHANNON	(*painting*) There she is, returning to me. See her perfect skin, the smooth, spared breast, yes, I can touch perfection again, yes, her supple limbs holding me, yes, the apples... (*beat*) Apples. Unh. This is awful. What have I made?
BEARDSLEY	(*slinking in around the tree, cane in hand*) It appears, a deciduous sapling.
SHANNON	A tree?!
BEARDSLEY	You say that as if it were a *bad* thing.

SHANNON Beardsley. I've wrecked it. I'm trying, trying to go back.

BEARDSLEY Yes, the Lincolnshire farmer thirsts to show devotion by the blisters on his palms.

SHANNON There's this awful rupture between what I can imagine—in here—and what I can scrawl on the canvas. How can I broach it?

BEARDSLEY Stop "trying." I only sweated on my sickbed. You've been led to a tree, so paint the tree. Release, thrill yourself. Feel it, here.

— • —

Fast.

BROWN (*stopped at a painting*) Here.

RICKETTS Absolutely not.

(BEARDSLEY (*grabbing SHANNON*) And here.)

BROWN Cézanne is a well-regarded–

RICKETTS Failure.

(BEARDSLEY (*grabbing SHANNON*) And yes. Finally, here.)

BROWN Ricketts...

(BEARDSLEY Feel it.)

RICKETTS This isn't painting.

(BEARDSLEY Release a sensual salvo of brush-strokes.)

BROWN It will prove very popular.

RICKETTS Look at it, Brown. Truly look at it and tell me: Can you find any trace of beauty?

(BEARDSLEY (*as SHANNON paints*) Surrender, Shannon.)

BROWN   It has colour and form.

RICKETTS   So does my bedspread.

(BEARDSLEY   Paint its essence.)

RICKETTS   It's geometry, not art. The composition is hackneyed, the perspective is laughable. Pink crushed against yellow may be fashionable on a party dress, but on a mountain it's nothing but the ejaculations of an untidy and abortive movement.

BROWN   You're out of touch, man. The entire art world admires / his work–

RICKETTS   I am not in fashion's thrall. No one alive knows more about European art. I am a painter, designer, critic and collector. I illustrated all of Oscar Wilde's books...

BROWN   All? What about that Aubrey Beardsley–

RICKETTS   But one!

(BEARDSLEY   Yes!)

RICKETTS   (*angina*) All but one of his bloody books!

(BEARDSLEY   A breakthrough tree.)

BROWN   Are you all right?

RICKETTS   No!

(BEARDSLEY   An expressionistic tree.)

RICKETTS   Due to that cartilaginous baron of beef you forced me to eat.

BROWN   I hardly–

RICKETTS   Compounded by the paintings you foist at me!

(BEARDSLEY   A thoroughly modern tree.)

RICKETTS   Next you'll say Van Gogh–

BROWN   Van Gogh is a great artist.

> *RICKETTS scoffs in disappointment.*

That man suffered–

RICKETTS   We all suffer. I suffer. How I suffer.

(BEARDSLEY   Beautiful.)

(SHANNON   Yes?)

RICKETTS   A matter of interest for doctors, not critics. The question remains: are his paintings good. I see a brush stroke like macaroni in tomato sauce, and I know they are not.

(BEARDSLEY   It's the way they're making trees these days.)

RICKETTS   I am trying to build you the best collection of Old Masters in North America.

(BEARDSLEY   Look forward, man – they're waiting for you.)

BROWN   You know why most people visit our national gallery?

(BEARDSLEY   The future.)

BROWN   It isn't your Canalettos. They come for the stuffed fish.

(SHANNON   Yes?)

RICKETTS   There are no stuffed–

BROWN   Upstairs in the Natural History Exhibition with stuffed bears and the rifles that shot them.

(BEARDSLEY   You're finally free.)

BROWN   When they loaned it all to Chicago, our own attendance dropped to twenty visitors a day.

(**SHANNON**   I feel it.)

BROWN   Twenty people! Folks'd rather gawk at a huge salmon than a portrait of some sausage-fingered duchess.

RICKETTS   This is a civilisation we're building, not a hunting lodge.

(**BEARDSLEY**   You've surrendered to the storm of progress.)

BROWN   I know. I'm just telling you what I'm up against.

(**BEARDSLEY**   You'll arrive late to the party; make a proper entrance.)

BROWN   We need paintings that will be popular. Relevant. Modern.

(**BEARDSLEY**   The New Expressionist.)

RICKETTS   Exactly. That's why the painting by Piero–

BROWN   Piero di Cosimo is four hundred years old!

— • —

SHANNON   The party, yes. I've arrived.

BEARDSLEY   Now you know what you must do?

SHANNON   Have a show?

BEARDSLEY   No. Die. Die, I say!

SHANNON   Rather extreme.

BEARDSLEY   It's not enough to be a visionary; you must also be remembered.

SHANNON   I'm not a visionary.

BEARDSLEY   You're seeing me, aren't you?

SHANNON   Does seem that way.

BEARDSLEY   Death will salvage you.

— • —

RICKETTS   Wait till you see it. A gorgeous Apollo. And Sibyl.

BROWN   Sibyl. You think people–

RICKETTS   Providing crucial links in the collection between Titian and later work of, say, Bellotto.

(SHANNON   (*climbing the ladder*) A heroic death?)

BROWN   How much.

(BEARDSLEY   Certainly. Up you go.)

RICKETTS   Ten thousand pounds.

(BEARDSLEY   Higher.)

BROWN   That's twice my budget!

(SHANNON   Oh God.)

RICKETTS   It will be a travesty if the National Gallery of Canada does not acquire it.

(SHANNON   Too high.)

(BEARDSLEY   Rarified air, Shannon.)

BROWN   Reconcile yourself.

(BEARDSLEY   A final breath, then fame forever. Jump!)

(SHANNON   Uhhhh... uhhhhh!)

(KATHERINE   (*entering SHANNON's world*) Shannon, stop! Beardsley...)

RICKETTS   Middlebrow.

(**SHANNON**   Michael!)

BROWN   We don't have the money.

(**BEARDSLEY**   Shit.)

(**SHANNON**   Help me!)

(**KATHERINE**   Help yourself and get down.)

RICKETTS   (*walking off*) Then I'll go and get it from your King of Canada.

(**BEARDSLEY**   Jump!)

BROWN   King.

(**KATHERINE**   No.)

BROWN   Mackenzie King?

(**BEARDSLEY**   Yes!)

BROWN   (*following RICKETTS off*) You think our Prime Minister cares about *art*?!

— • —

KATHERINE   Stop trying to kill everything!

BEARDSLEY   *Moi?* A gaunt, febrile creature? I'm merely fixing him into the agate of history.

KATHERINE   With this as your legacy? Fay will hate it. Die and he'll only burn it.

SHANNON   But how else can I compete with the past? It's been around *so long*.

KATHERINE   But it's powerless when forgotten. The world has changed; it's been hit on the head. Keep painting and outlive them all.

SHANNON (*descending*) "Hit on the head," that's, that's very good. Conversation, Michael – thrilling ephemera! Wait until Ricketts returns, he'll be so happy to see you.

BEARDSLEY I don't think so.

SHANNON Even you, Beardsley. He's craved this so long...

KATHERINE Shannon, dear, we're dead.

SHANNON Oh. Oh. I forgot.

BEARDSLEY Helios is wringing the last of his light. Come, Michael.

SHANNON But Edith. Poor Edith!

EDITH (*calling offstage*) Coming, Shannon, it's all right.

SHANNON (*still in his fantasy*) You left her?

KATHERINE Swallowed by the past, exquisite tranquility.

> *EDITH enters bringing on the basin and sponge. She goes for SHANNON, blind to his fantasy.*

SHANNON Poor Edith!

EDITH Oh Shannon, what a mess. (*covering it*) Fay would be sickened.

SHANNON ...Fifty fifty fifty fifty hear sixty...

(KATHERINE Don't let death take you.)

EDITH Give me your hand, we'll tidy you up.

(BEARDSLEY Consider an exit. Elysian fields are infinitely better than *Michael* Fields! (*A dog barks.*) Come, Whym Chow, come!)

> *BEARDSLEY exits leaving KATHERINE to watch EDITH care for SHANNON.*

SHANNON	Michael... life... spilled.
EDITH	Yes, Shannon, she's gone. You just keep forgetting.
(**KATHERINE**	(*caressing EDITH's hair, although EDITH doesn't notice*) "The world was on us pressing sore / My Love and I took hands and swore / Against the world, to be...")
SHANNON	Gone.
(**KATHERINE**	"...Poets and lovers ever more.")
EDITH	What are you looking at? Oh. Fay. I didn't hear you come in. He was having one of his little visions. How was the auction? Did you buy anything for the New World?
RICKETTS	(*having entered*) No we did not.
SHANNON	Gone. Twenty-five, twenty-five, hear twenty, twenty, twenty...
RICKETTS	I'm going to Canada.
EDITH	Fay, that's impossible!
RICKETTS	I've already booked passage. I'm seeking special funds.
EDITH	For the painting?
RICKETTS	Yes, for the painting.
SHANNON	Twenty-five, twenty-five, thirty, thirty...
EDITH	I must say, your logic is extremely tenuous.
RICKETTS	It's perfectly sound.
EDITH	You're going to Canada to beg money to buy them a painting by Piero della Francesca–
RICKETTS	Piero di Cosimo! Please!

EDITH   A forgotten Italian painter, so that what, you might hang it in your home for a week–

RICKETTS   I won't even need a week–

EDITH   ...In the hopes of inducing an epiphany in Charles here?

RICKETTS   Exactly.

SHANNON   Forty. Forty.

EDITH   It's preposterous.

RICKETTS   (*beat*) I'll wash him, Edith.

EDITH   You have sacrificed so much already.

RICKETTS   Clearly not enough. You're tired. Go.

EDITH   Why do you think a painting will change anything?

RICKETTS   Because it did once before.

EDITH   But why would you–

RICKETTS   Because I am desperate! Now, may we have a modicum of privacy in our own home?

EDITH   (*pause, exiting*) Perhaps a walk. To suffer the perils of enforced leisure.

SHANNON   Edie!

RICKETTS   Shh. Here. Arms. Let's clean you up, you little rapscallion.

SHANNON   Painting. Trees.

RICKETTS   Trees. Yes, we have many paintings of trees.

SHANNON   No! Llllll. Look.

RICKETTS	I see them, Chubbs: trees and cities, peasants and gods. And one lonely shepherdess.
SHANNON	See? Dead.
RICKETTS	Of course. Anyone worth collecting is dead – except us, of course. We'll soon find the rest of you, Shannon. Because I've found the Piero.
SHANNON	Peee-ero.
(PUVIS	(*offstage*) *Charmante!*)
RICKETTS	I contacted the Bensons, it hasn't sold. You'll set eyes on it again. It'll fix everything.
SHANNON	Peeeeeeee veeeee...
(PUVIS	(*offstage*) *Charmante jeunesse!*)
RICKETTS	Piero, yes. Canada also has no memory, but I'm changing that. I am building a culture capable of appreciating us.
SHANNON	(*urgently grabbing him*) Dead. Pulling. P-! P-!
RICKETTS	My dear, dear fellow. I know you're there. I know you're punishing me, fled into your strange worlds, your crippled language. I know you can do better. I know this because I made you. What *you* don't know is that when I'm gone there will be nobody left who still believes in the best of you. You'll be lost like a sunken city. Is spite enough reason to waste your life? I am going to Canada to meet the Prime Minister. When I come back... please have more of you waiting for me.

> *RICKETTS exits. SHANNON addresses the audience.*

SHANNON	And so he continued, clinging to hope, to the life he saw in me. Who was Piero? I'd forgotten him, as I'm quite sure you have. Ricketts!

SHANNON stops to look in amazement at a painting. Lights swiftly shift.

10.

The home of Puvis de Chavannes. SHANNON, young, looks up to a painting in awe.

SHANNON   Ricketts! Psst!

RICKETTS   (*entering, young and scratching, calling back*) *Un moment, Monsieur....* What is it?

SHANNON   Look at that sun. Who could paint a sky like that?

RICKETTS   Ah. Ah! Piero di Cosimo.

SHANNON   It's so real, blazing there. The Louvre today had nothing like this. And Puvis here bought it for his own house!

PUVIS   (*offstage*) *Ça va?*

RICKETTS   *Absolument! Shannon est un peu ivre, c'est tout!*

SHANNON   What did you say?

RICKETTS   You have *got* to learn French.

SHANNON   First I'll learn to paint like that.

RICKETTS   (*beat*) Yes. Yes. Now you see. Do you know the story here?

SHANNON   It tells a story?

RICKETTS   Piero didn't just paint a sky; he painted drama. See here, it's Apollo and Sibyl.

SHANNON   You be Apollo.

RICKETTS   Well, he says to her, "Sibyl, you beauteous wench, you send my heart and loins galloping. As a token of my undying devotion, I will give you one wish."

SHANNON	(*playing, as they copy the pose of the painting*) "Ummm. All right."
RICKETTS	So you take a handful of sand...
SHANNON	(*miming*) Right. I take a handful of sand and I say, "Apollo, I... I would like this handful of sand..."
RICKETTS	No! You say, "Apollo, I want as many *birthdays* as are grains of sand in my hand."
SHANNON	Ah. Well. "Give me this many birthdays, you kind and lovely man."
RICKETTS	He's a god. The *sun* god.
SHANNON	Yes. Of course, the sun!
RICKETTS	Then he asks her, "Are you sure that's your wish?"
SHANNON	"That is my wish."
RICKETTS	"Very well, Sibyl, immortality is yours."
SHANNON	That's the moment, right there, captured forever.
RICKETTS	"Now, you ravishing prophetess, you must seal the bargain."
SHANNON	"If you insist, Apollo."
	They lean in close to one another, about to kiss. Just then, PUVIS enters in his great cloak.
PUVIS	*Quelle charmante jeunesse.*
RICKETTS	(*jumping up*) *Monsieur, Shannon est épris de votre peinture.*
SHANNON	Tell him I will paint glorious suns like that.
RICKETTS	*Il veut peindre comme ça.*
PUVIS	*C'est très difficile.*

SHANNON I uh, *Je ne care-ay pas!* I have *seen-ay le lumière!*

PUVIS (*taking SHANNON and leading him off*) *Je peux te montrer un chemin. Il sera difficile, mais si tu suis mes conseils, tu deviendras un grand artiste.*

SHANNON *Oui, Monsieur*, whatever you're saying.

> As RICKETTS stays to admire the painting, PUVIS leads SHANNON off.

RICKETTS *Charmante jeunesse.*

> SHANNON reappears, watching RICKETTS admiring the painting.

SHANNON Through my eye, to my heart. And so, he thought, if the beauty of that painting could transform a twenty year-old dullard into a refined æsthete, it might work again nearly fifty years later.

> PUVIS removes his cloak, revealing William Lyon Mackenzie KING beneath. SHANNON may remain on stage, reading the journal.

II.

> Lights shift. RICKETTS still studies the painting. KING studies him. BROWN skulks.

KING So what d'you think?

RICKETTS It's... novel. Extremely... novel. Brush work on the uh... collar here, exceptional. You can see the resemblance.

KING Mother was everything to me.

RICKETTS I understand. My own, she, well...

KING Yes.

RICKETTS When I was fourteen.

KING   So young.

RICKETTS   I felt as old as the earth.

BROWN   So you find comfort in your painter-friend Shannon.

KING   Oh ho ho, and who is she?

RICKETTS   *Charles* Shannon.

KING   Oh.

RICKETTS   "Comfort" is perhaps over-...

BROWN   You've lived together how long? Ricketts?

RICKETTS   (*pause*) Almost fifty years. We met in art school.

BROWN   Very comfortable.

RICKETTS   Mr. Mackenzie King, you may be interested to know of an exhibition we're mounting in London: "Italian Painting, 1200-1900." It opens New Year's day. Mussolini and the Pope have promised us unbelievable paintings. All great countries of the world will lend works.

KING   Will Canada?

RICKETTS   Oh yes, a Botticelli, a Tintoretto and a, a, a...

BROWN   Cariani...

RICKETTS   Cariani, yes, all purchases I made for the gallery. If we bought the Piero, Canada would be among the stars.

KING   Not that often a new country sends beautiful things back to the old. Usually the other way around. Except, of course, when we ship our young men across the seas to die.

RICKETTS   Sir, please, they don't *all*–

KING   I know, just Armistice Day, it's on my mind. Have to speak at the cenotaph. Sad day.

RICKETTS   A happy one, sir, if we acquire the Piero. Quite unlike anything else in the gallery.

BROWN   Actually, you've gotten us a lot of Italians.

RICKETTS   Those are Venice. This is Florence.

BROWN   Only the desperate resort to geography.

RICKETTS   I brought you something, Brown. (*producing a bar*) Lovely Lydia's Lavender Soap.

KING   Well isn't that nice?

RICKETTS   Why don't you go lubricate your wife?

BROWN   You'd do well to keep it. Our winter air is most inhospitable. Sir, thank-you again. We'll be drawing up gallery plans within the month.

RICKETTS   ...Plans?

BROWN   I received special funds just yesterday, toward the erection of a new and separate gallery.

KING   Lovely place, near the river.

BROWN   Free of fish.

KING   The building, not the river. Gonna cost a King's ransom, but hey. Get it? King's ransom?

RICKETTS   I've arrived too late.

BROWN   (*laughing along*) You can feast on scraps for a change. Good morning, sir.

        BROWN exits. RICKETTS lingers.

RICKETTS   Sir, about the Piero...

KING	They nude?
RICKETTS	Apollo and–? No, sir.
KING	You keep buying us nudes. The last one, with the lamb and those two naked boys. What was it?
RICKETTS	The Christ Child and Infant John the Baptist?
KING	Yeah. The flack we got in Question Period for that one.
RICKETTS	Piero's painting chastely depicts the moment Apollo grants Sibyl immortality.
KING	I like the theme: bold medicine for the limpets who clog Parliament Hill, whingeing how the stocks won't recover – the stocks will bloody well recover. I see the bigger picture. I have forces aiding me, oh yes: the dead. Do you hear them?
RICKETTS	I haven't been listening.
KING	There's only a sheer membrane concealing them, thinner than the canvasses you buy us. I should tell you, Ricketts, there are ways of reaching your mother.
RICKETTS	I don't think that's how the dead speak to us.
KING	Oh? Then how do they?
RICKETTS	Through... through art. Through the beauty they leave behind.
KING	Most of us don't leave much of that.
RICKETTS	Most of us are forgotten. That's why if you want a monument, this, this painting...
KING	What about the painting.
RICKETTS	I too require a special grant. I think it can be had for ten thousand. I must stress how important Piero–

KING   Dollars?

RICKETTS   Pounds, sir.

KING   (*pause*) How big is it?

RICKETTS   ...Adequate... sir.

KING   (*absorbing himself in his speech notes*) You already get your budget.

RICKETTS   This painting costs twice our budget. We'd be out of the market for two years–

KING   Then you'd better not buy it.

RICKETTS   Sir...

KING   I just spent twenty thousand dollars to get this bloody gallery off the ground.

RICKETTS   You build it, sir, make sure it isn't empty.

KING   What've you been buying us?

RICKETTS   Some wonderful paintings. But you need a, a star. The Louvre is nothing without the Mona Lisa. The British Museum is practically standing on the Elgin Marbles. What will your new National Gallery of Canada be known for?

KING   We'll find out. But right now I have to speak–

RICKETTS   At the cenotaph, yes. You will talk of the dead, of remembrance. But tell me, sir, how *do* we remember? Between the swings of time's pendulum, between joy and destruction, we embody our passion in works of art. They enrich experience centuries ahead and give us a foretaste of permanence. Through them we realise a kind of immortality – the only one truly ours.

KING   Why do you care?

RICKETTS I know what beautiful things can do.

KING Oh? And what can beauty do?

RICKETTS I met Charles Shannon at art school. He was eighteen, in from the country. I was just sixteen, a terrified, awkward orphan. Together we went to galleries, bought things, surrounded ourselves in beauty. It refined our conversation, our ideas, our... our desires. Where will a man find such inspiration in Canada but for you?

KING I doubt Canada has many men like you, Ricketts.

RICKETTS We are all the same in our need for beauty.

KING Very true. I'll consider it.

RICKETTS But why wait?

KING I must go, I'm late.

RICKETTS All worthy men are, chasing the past. Please, sir, there is such little time–

KING I know. There is indeed very little time. Go home. Buy us the painting. I will back you.

RICKETTS Mister Mackenzie King. You will not regret–

KING (*waving him off*) Nice meeting you, Ricketts. My regards to your uh...

> *RICKETTS leaves. Rising wind. KING grabs his cloak, pins a poppy to it and buttons up. As SHANNON pulls a clipping from the journal, KING speaks over the howling wind.*

"Ladies and gentlemen. We gather today across this great nation for a most sombre task: to remember. Why? The Great War's shadow has receded; the sun shines again, bleaching the bones of our brothers. We know such horrors could never be repeated. But I tell you, without remembrance, we shall always stumble. So let us remember those citizens who have carried us this far. Let us honour their suffering."

He falters, ignoring his notes. SHANNON, meanwhile, drops the journal and clipping, returning to paint.

Such suffering, yes. We are surrounded by the dead. And yet the sun stubbornly shines.

(SHANNON   Risen again.)

KING   It's time for the citizen who believes in beauty, not war.

(SHANNON   The new artist!)

KING   Who embraces where we come from so we may know where we are going.

(SHANNON   Who flies blind!)

KING   For without memory, we don't deserve the civilization others have built for us.

(SHANNON   Alive! Alive and free!)

KING   Without memory, we are sure to lose our footing.

12.

Through the sound of a storm, SHANNON paints with his new-found flamboyance.

SHANNON   Blow! Crack! Howl! The storm has come! I am the rough gusts of change! I am the wind blowing from Paradise, blowing to the future! Nothing can overtake me – I have dropped the past, shattered and forgotten. Nothing stands in my way. Nothing can stand!

RICKETTS   *(entering, a big coat and hat masking him)* Shannon?

*SHANNON pushes RICKETTS to the ground.
The instant he falls, the storm stops and the space
transforms back into the drawing room.*

RICKETTS   Charles! What are you–?

SHANNON   (*shocked by the sight of RICKETTS*) Uhhnnn! You!
Broke!

RICKETTS   Yes, it's me – I'm back. What a hideous
aberration. We'll evict this immediately.

SHANNON   No! Crack! Blow winds! Crack your cheeks!

RICKETTS   "Cheeks?" Did you just...?

SHANNON   Crack!

HOLMES   (*entering from within the house*) Welcome home,
Charles. I've been waiting for you.

RICKETTS   He just quoted Shakespeare! Amazing.

SHANNON   Wrecked!

RICKETTS   Go on, "cataracts and hurricanoes..." Dare say he
didn't recognise me.

HOLMES   Your Eskimo fashions.

RICKETTS   Yes, winter is damnably cold in Canada. But what
a triumph.

EDITH   (*entering*) Oh Fay, welcome back.

RICKETTS   Edith, my light, we're on the cusp. He's quoting
Shakespeare!

SHANNON   Fffffaaaahhhhh... fifty fifty fifty...

EDITH   Is he now.

RICKETTS   (*of painting*) This psychic leakage clearly distresses
him.

EDITH	You're wrong; he has been happy.
RICKETTS	Then why'd he quote Lear on the heath and not Romeo at the balcony?
EDITH	Leave it, he lives here as much as you do.
RICKETTS	Only beautiful things in this house, Edith, that is the prescription for recovery. Now please lead the avant-garde to his bedroom.
EDITH	Go rest yourself. Canada has clearly addled your senses.

> *EDITH takes SHANNON off. RICKETTS continues to HOLMES, dismantling SHANNON's work.*

RICKETTS	I'm healthy as an ox! Pinch my skin: sea air for a week, strolls around the deck.... Holmes, I feel I should squeeze your handsome form. There, I did it!
HOLMES	Charles.
RICKETTS	I trust the Italian Exhibition gallops apace. I talked to Canada's Prime Minister about it, he's very impressed. When I think of the days you were our office boy at the Vale Press...
HOLMES	Manager.
RICKETTS	...How far you've come, it's a source of great pride to have been such an influence.
HOLMES	Manager, Charles.
RICKETTS	Mm?
HOLMES	I was the manager of the Vale Press. Not the office boy.
RICKETTS	Of course. And now look at us, changing history in our respective posts.

HOLMES   Have you read the papers?

RICKETTS   My dear boy, I have lived these shipboard days in
            glorious, timeless solitude, knowing all the while
            that I would be thrust into *le monde* as soon as
            I arrived.

HOLMES   Yes, well.

RICKETTS   (*bruised rear*) Little did I realise I'd be thrown "*on*"
            le monde.

HOLMES   Yes, well there's news.

RICKETTS   I got the ten thousand pounds! I am to furnish
            Canada with its immortal Sibyl. But first I'll bring
            it here, for Shannon. It will snap his skull into...
            (*angina*) ...oh dear. Lucidity.

HOLMES   Ricketts. Something has happened.

RICKETTS   Then *tell* me, Holmes. I'm all ears.

HOLMES   You know the crash in the markets...

RICKETTS   What market. Covent Garden?

HOLMES   The stock market.

RICKETTS   Oh yes, they were muttering about it on the ship.
            When will people learn, if you must invest, invest
            in art. I'll change before going to Duveen's to
            arrange shipping. Will you come?

HOLMES   There's no point going to Duveen's.

RICKETTS   My dear boy, were you not listening?

HOLMES   (*handing over a telegram*) It was wired through my
            office. For some reason they thought you worked
            there.

RICKETTS   Understandably, dear boy. I do practically– (*pause,
            reading*) Brown. Brown is – No. I met the Prime
            Minister. I persuaded him.

HOLMES	The markets are not recovering, Charles.
RICKETTS	Are you coming to Duveen's or not.
HOLMES	Charles, stop. There's no point.
RICKETTS	"Do not buy Cosmo. No funds." "Cosmo." He can't even spell it.
HOLMES	A hitch in the wire.
RICKETTS	No. This is Brown's revenge.
HOLMES	I doubt he orchestrated a stock crash–
RICKETTS	I wouldn't put it past him. Destroying my glory...
HOLMES	"Glory?" It's only a Cosimo.
RICKETTS	"Only...!"
HOLMES	He's hardly a great. Hell, we've got ten or so at the National.
RICKETTS	(*angina*) You arrogant little prick. The "director" of England's gallery.
HOLMES	You gave it–
RICKETTS	I know I gave it up! Did I have the gift of prophesy? Did I know know my life would collapse in such spectacular ruin? And you. I remember when you were an office boy!
HOLMES	I was your / manager–
RICKETTS	You were a boy! A lovely, handsome, eager protégé. And now I look at you, stuffed and pompous and knighted and, and, and *married*. You break my heart. Swaggering around Trafalgar Square like you own the place. Ten Cosimos and half stored in the bloody basement. What are they to you, "Sir" Charles? What did you know about painting before I made you?

(*collapsing melodramatically*) The worst mistake of my life, letting the post go. And now I've lost the painting.

HOLMES   Not quite. We're going to buy it, the National Gallery. Should have it in time to unveil at the Italian Exhibition.

RICKETTS   Ah.

SHANNON   (*entering*) Lllloud... halls...

HOLMES   You have many projects still. Your theatre design, your own painting...

RICKETTS   Lear himself. Good choice, Shannon. Say something more. Please, Chubbs. Please.

SHANNON   Sixty sixty sixty sixty, hear sixty-five...

> *EDITH enters, wooden bowl and spoon in hand. RICKETTS extricates himself from SHANNON and goes to remove a painting from the wall.*

RICKETTS   This Masaccio. We found it in a jumble-bin, bought for the price of a good frame. So young. We were so lucky in those days.

HOLMES   A lovely painting.

RICKETTS   Sell it.

EDITH   Fay, no.

SHANNON   Ehhhnnn!

HOLMES   This is a bad time to be–

RICKETTS   The bloody Canadians have cheated me and I am broke.

SHANNON   Nnnnnnnn...

RICKETTS Could you also inquire whether Chester Beatty might purchase our Persian drawings.

EDITH What's happened to you?

RICKETTS We have four, all of them up to his standards.

SHANNON Uhhnnn!

EDITH Shhhhh...

HOLMES It's the best collection in England. You've gone without meals, scoured the continent–

EDITH It is all you have.

RICKETTS The rich sell without demur. I am poor; why shouldn't I?

HOLMES You could reduce your costs. Consider sending him somewhere.

SHANNON Ehhhhhhnnnnnn!

RICKETTS Impossible.

HOLMES You are hæmorrhaging money – and for what? An army of doctors to smack his pillows? He will never be anything more than a kindly and listless ghost.

RICKETTS He spoke beautiful poetry. I heard him. He is on the cusp.

HOLMES Of what?

RICKETTS Returning.

SHANNON Nnnnnnnnnnnnn. Nooo.

EDITH So you sell everything. So he gets better – then what?

RICKETTS   (*giving HOLMES the painting*) Then he and I will have a proper conversation. That most ephemeral of arts. Now the Italian exhibition: I'm going to hang it.

HOLMES   Charles. We have a committee to / do the work–

RICKETTS   Yes, men of such calculated stupidity they could sap an army's strength.

EDITH   You're in poor health.

RICKETTS   And when I die, the things I know will die with me. It will be the greatest exhibition ever. Nobody can hang it better than me. Not even you.

HOLMES   If it's money you need–

RICKETTS   I need to hang those paintings! To lift the Birth of Venus in her place. To make Fra Angelico and Mantegna comfortable. And yes, to show Shannon his Apollo again. Don't say anything. I'll come to the gallery tomorrow.

HOLMES   I should probably come here.

RICKETTS   No. Whenever you enter this room, Holmes, it's with bad news.

HOLMES   (*passing EDITH*) How do you stand it.

> HOLMES *exits with the Masaccio. SHANNON is busy with his painting. RICKETTS exhausted.*

SHANNON   Storm. Look. Look!

RICKETTS   Yes. Yes it is a storm. Another young man has turned on me.

EDITH   He's only trying to do what's best. You should listen–

RICKETTS	Quit cleaning, Edith. I can't bear your constant movement.
EDITH	I know. Only beautiful things. I do understand you. Well, Fay, I'm no longer beautiful. I am half a person, half a name. Even you have stopped calling me "Field" because there's no "Michael" to complete it. Her loss, Fay – her loss is lodged in me, stopping my breath, incessantly pressing on my heart. It is taking years. I expect solitude is something to be learned, like Greek.
RICKETTS	How do you comfort yourself?
EDITH	Memories. I read, the books we wrote together. Her voice is in there, mingled with mine.
RICKETTS	I have my journals. You think Shannon might one day read them?
EDITH	I doubt it, Fay.
SHANNON	(*the empty spot on the wall*) A hole. A hole up there.
RICKETTS	We must hope, Edith. Why else are you here?
EDITH	To cheer him, as butterflies cheer a hollow forest. But I can't transform him.
RICKETTS	I can. I already made him once.
EDITH	No, Fay, you didn't. That was a lie you told each other. Shannon made himself. He had the talent, he did the work. He chose the path.
RICKETTS	But I led him to it.
EDITH	And now you're chasing him through the trees, like Apollo after Daphne – "Shannon, Shannon, come back, be mine." He's dodging you the only way he can. He'd rather turn into a dull stump than be caught by you.
RICKETTS	He is trying, I see it.

EDITH	Stop and he'll stop. Let him go and he'll return to you.
	EDITH exits.
RICKETTS	Chubbs? Applesauce.
SHANNON	Mmm!
RICKETTS	(*tenderly feeding him*) Yes, mm. Look at you, Chubbs, such a smooth face.
SHANNON	Smooth...
RICKETTS	And me a dull, cracked canvas.
SHANNON	(*chuckling*) Not a *c-canvas*...
RICKETTS	Yes, I'll be rolled up and stashed away. I'll arrange for you to be cared for: Egypt will go first. Japan second, the Puvis de Chavannes third. They'll sell the Old Masters last, only if necessary.
SHANNON	No...
RICKETTS	It may be necessary, Chubbs. You found the secret to perpetual youth.
SHANNON	So sad...
RICKETTS	We worked so hard, harder than anyone. But I told us the wrong stories. Where are you now, Shannon? Where are you?
SHANNON	T-too high.

13.

*Gallery, a storm outside. The "Ghosts,"
(KATHERINE, WILDE and BEARDSLEY)
enter. RICKETTS addresses the Ghosts as workers
hanging the paintings. SHANNON alone sees them
as Ghosts, but RICKETTS and HOLMES dismiss
him as delirious.*

RICKETTS	Too high. It's Venus!
SHANNON	(*to the ghosts*) You're dead...
RICKETTS	Botticelli never wanted us to grovel at her feet.
SHANNON	(*to the ghosts*) No...
RICKETTS	(*ignoring SHANNON*) She's painted so you might look beauty in the eye.
SHANNON	Ghosts!
RICKETTS	Settle, Shannon. They're only the workmen.
HOLMES	(*entering*) Ricketts...
RICKETTS	Holmes! Truth and beauty!
HOLMES	Let the men go. It's New Year's Eve.
SHANNON	(*to the Ghosts*) I know why.
RICKETTS	And you open tomorrow. Do you want the eyes of the future admiring blank walls?
HOLMES	The men'll be back by sunrise.
RICKETTS	Ha! Precisely when they'll be staggering into bed.
HOLMES	They have families waiting for them.
SHANNON	(*to the Ghosts*) Go away!
RICKETTS	(*embarrassed*) Shannon... (*beat*) Go then, go chew geese with your wives.
SHANNON	(*to the Ghosts, who remain*) Go chew geese!
HOLMES	You look awful. I knew this was too much for you.
RICKETTS	I'll rest soon enough, dear boy. Look. A wall of Botticellis, never in the same room before. Even the artist himself never saw what we now see.

HOLMES	There are certain advantages to the Twentieth Century after all.
RICKETTS	I wouldn't go *that* far.
SHANNON	(*to the Ghosts*) Go! Far!
RICKETTS	Now leave. I'll hang this Piero myself. Then I'll take Shannon home.
SHANNON	(*to the Ghosts*) Leave us!
HOLMES	Happy New Year.
RICKETTS	My regards to your wife.

> *HOLMES exits. In RICKETTS's world, he's now alone with SHANNON.*

RICKETTS	What's the matter with you tonight? I swear you *want* to shock strangers. I'll hang our painting. You wait.
(**KATHERINE**	Curious, that tendency to touch a bandaged wound, to see if it will hurt.)
SHANNON	You can't take him.
(**OSCAR**	Settle, old man. He can't hear us.)
(**BEARDSLEY**	Yet.)
RICKETTS	(*absorbed in hanging the painting*) We're not taking anything, Chubbs, just wait.
(**BEARDSLEY**	When is he coming?)
(**KATHERINE**	Won't be long now.)

> *The painting hung, RICKETTS is still up the ladder.*

RICKETTS	There. It's up, Chubbers. If you want it.

(**OSCAR**   Look back, Charles.)

(**BEARDSLEY**   Over your shoulder.)

(**KATHERINE**   Turn.)

SHANNON   No.

RICKETTS   Do what you like, Chubbs.

(**KATHERINE**   You're almost there.)

RICKETTS   I won't make you.

(**BEARDSLEY**   You're on the threshold.)

(**KATHERINE**   Turn and look back / one last time.)

(**OSCAR**   One last time, turn and be sure.)

RICKETTS   It's up to you now.

(**BEARDSLEY**   Turn and shatter everything.)

> *SHANNON now turns to regard the painting. After he does, he no longer sees the Ghosts. RICKETTS struggles to temper his hope and excitement.*

SHANNON   Peeeee... ling.

RICKETTS   Yes! She's peeling.

SHANNON   Old.

RICKETTS   Well? Sibyl made her bargain with Apollo to live forever.

SHANNON   But... she forgot.

RICKETTS   That's right. Sibyl forgot to ask for eternal youthfulness.

SHANNON   Apollo...

RICKETTS Yes, and Apollo that wily letch, he'd only grant her that if she'd be his mistress.

SHANNON But I couldn't.

RICKETTS You couldn't, no. And so Apollo left time to ravage her.

SHANNON Old stories.

RICKETTS People believed them once.

SHANNON I believed them.

RICKETTS Yes.

SHANNON This was his, the old man's.

RICKETTS Puvis de Chavannes. He owned it.

SHANNON His dusty cloak. Yes. I remember. Said I was an artist.

RICKETTS He was right!

SHANNON We ate oysters, yes. Paris, a bed, a b-bath.

RICKETTS To drown the fleas!

SHANNON Fleas! *Charmante*! Paintings, roses, emerald roses. The garden. The tree.

RICKETTS You see it?

SHANNON Up there? I see the whole world. That painting. Charles Ricketts, it's all in me.

A deluge of apples falls from above to the ground.

14.

The distant sound of a dog barking. Birds chirp. RICKETTS is up the tree, sixteen. He throws an apple plucked from the tree at SHANNON.

SHANNON Ricketts! Come out of that tree, you'll break your neck.

RICKETTS Go away.

SHANNON We're just having a laugh. You're such a know-it-all in class, the lads leap at the chance to tease you.

RICKETTS So I don't know the body. I know art.

SHANNON Come, you've never seen one before?

RICKETTS All stood up like that? No. (*beat*) Had you?

SHANNON Sure. Guess 'cause I grew up in Lincolnshire, the farms, I saw my share...

RICKETTS Well if I ever saw one, I certainly didn't know what it was *for*. I never really went to school before here. Too busy travelling the continent with my mother.

SHANNON Folks have them on the continent too...

RICKETTS Ha, ha. Can't be I'm the only one who didn't know we had that... what d'you call it?

SHANNON A skeleton. How else did you suppose you were held up?

RICKETTS I don't know. With terracotta clay, I suppose. (*off SHANNON's laugh*) We artists needn't concern ourselves with our insides.

SHANNON I'm not an artist. Engraving's a trade, not an art.

RICKETTS	You don't seriously plan to be an engraver? How dull.
SHANNON	It'll support a family.
RICKETTS	I've seen your classwork. You're good. Better than those cretins.
SHANNON	You're too cruel.
RICKETTS	My affections are all buried with my mother. She died when I was fourteen. And now I am sixteen. Today is my birthday.
SHANNON	Felicitations. Will you see your family?
RICKETTS	It would be as absurd as for a dove to be among sea-gulls. Father dead, sister in Germany I think. Cinders, ashes, dust.
SHANNON	(*climbing up the ladder to join RICKETTS*) So what will you do tonight?
RICKETTS	Paint in my rooms by candlelight.
SHANNON	Paint?! Alone? No, I'll come for tea.
RICKETTS	You should move in. I've got a large bed.
SHANNON	I'm already lodging with Roger Fry.
RICKETTS	That talentless scribbler? A young fresh pimple. You'll never develop your genius with him.
SHANNON	I'm hardly a genius.
RICKETTS	You just need somebody to believe in you. Come to France with me.
SHANNON	I don't speak French.
RICKETTS	I do. See? I'm perfect for you.
SHANNON	You're funny.

RICKETTS   I don't care what anybody thinks. No genius ever did. See that sky? Titian's ripe clouds are resolving into the smudge of a Turner horizon. You see?

SHANNON   Yes...?

RICKETTS   You know the Gemini story?

SHANNON   Ricketts, I don't know anything.

RICKETTS   Castor and Pollux. One was immortal; the other was human and proved it by dying. Pollux, the immortal one, so loved Castor that he begged Zeus to let him take Castor's place, thereby allowing his beloved brother to live. Zeus was so touched by this devotion he allowed them to switch places every day; thus, each could enjoy a day alive, on earth, in exchange for a day dead among the gods. And so passing one another between earth and the heavens, Castor and Pollux would meet every sunset to embrace in the sky for a minute. They would talk and share thoughts and observations. And then...

> *RICKETTS kisses SHANNON. He then climbs down the ladder.*

With a kiss, one would depart for his turn on earth while the other would continue on up for his time among the gods. Can you see them, Shannon? The Titian clouds overhead? So perfect, so brief. That is beauty: a moment of harmony between opposites, hardly more enduring than music.

> *In ecstacy, RICKETTS suddenly stops, seized by a heart attack. RICKETTS subsides, descending as SHANNON remains at the top of the ladder watching the sunset. Veiled, HÉLÈNE joins the ghosts.*

SHANNON   That is beauty. Yes, I see it.

(OSCAR   Now?)

(**KATHERINE**   Now.)

(**RICKETTS**   (*finally seeing them*) Oscar. Has it come, my time
among the gods?)

(**BEARDSLEY**   A god – why Ricketts, you are too kind.)

(**RICKETTS**   You?!)

(**OSCAR**   Alas, the disappointments never cease.)

(**RICKETTS**   Where am I going?)

(**KATHERINE**   It's your turn, Fay. Be brave.)

(**RICKETTS**   *Maman?*)

(**HÉLÈNE**   Come with us.)

(**RICKETTS**   No, *Maman*, I can't. I'm not ready.)

(**BEARDSLEY**   You've had a whole life.)

(**RICKETTS**   I wasted it. I need more.)

(**HÉLÈNE**   You've had enough.)

(**RICKETTS**   I'm not good enough yet.)

(**KATHERINE**   You're done, Fay. You brought him back.)

(**OSCAR**   A proper sacrifice.)

(**RICKETTS**   Yes. And now he'll be so lonely.)

KATHERINE   Flame of Love...

They lead him off, singing in rich harmony.

(**QUARTET**   "I am desolate but do not weep;
A tongueless scream is on my breath for load;
And thou art in a little grave, deep, deep,
Scooped in my heart – such small abode
For thee, a spot so narrow where to keep
My all, in wood and stone the damps corrode.")

SHANNON   I see it, Ricketts, Such beauty there, in front of me.

15.

Drawing Room. SHANNON atop the ladder. Clipboard in hand, EDITH enters.

EDITH   Charles! Get down, you'll fall.

SHANNON   (*his reverie broken, rattled and shivering*) Ah? Oh dear... too high.

EDITH   Take it slow, that's it. Men! Fetch your bloody ladder!

SHANNON   Edith...

EDITH   Well? It's just the only way they'll listen. You said worse when you were lost to us.

SHANNON   (*carefully climbing down the ladder*) He's with them now, the dead I used to know.

EDITH   Fay? He is, but we're still here. Only it's time to leave.

SHANNON   He showed me the gods, then pushed me up to join them.

EDITH   Come, Charles.

SHANNON   Why?

EDITH   We have to go now.

SHANNON   Why do we love one thing and not another?

EDITH   The heart gets stubborn.

SHANNON   Time.

EDITH   You've had time, Charles.

SHANNON   Yes. (*shivering*) So cold in here.

EDITH   The movers left the front door open. Wouldn't be surprised if we die of chill. One last look then we're going. (*exiting*) Shut the door, you canvas-cracking heathens! You trying to kill us?

SHANNON   (*opening the box, gently lifting out the Tanagra*) He's gone. I'm left in your hands. So cold. The past... I dropped it.

>   *Shivering, SHANNON drops the Tanagra, shattering it.*

But life, I still have a great handful of life.

>   *He grabs a handful of dusty clay, crumbling it in his hands.*

Is there anything—from all our art and ideas and accomplishments that now lie fallow and rotting—anything you might take up and carry with you like an old man in your arms? Is there anything you might remember? Our techniques, our talent, our strange and novel love? A delicious feeling, love. It strikes you the way a rare Tanagra enters your life. The thrill shoots through you and in that instant of beholding a bit of terracotta moulded thousands of years ago by careful hands, holding it in your own, you feel your youth, a comparative brevity of existence. Knowing it can and shall be yours till you die. It makes you glad for your few years here on earth, that at least this time around, for this short time, you have been made of clay that is pliant and smooth, and warmed, warmed by something more than just the sun.

>   *The end.*

But Do Not Weep

marc desormeaux

photo by Kathryn Gaitens

— • —

Michael Lewis MacLennan began his writing career as a playwright on the West Coast. His first play *Beat the Sunset* (Playwrights Canada Press) won Vancouver's Jessie Richardson Award for Outstanding Emerging Playwright and the *Theatrum* National Playwriting Competition. His next major play *Grace* (Scirocco Drama) won the Theatre BC Canadian National Playwriting Competition. Other plays include *Leaning Over Railings, Come On!* and the libretto for the short opera *The Laurels*. His play *The Shooting Stage* (Playwrights Canada Press) won the Herman Voaden National Playwriting Award and was a finalist for the 2002 Governor General's Literary Award. *Last Romantics* was The Shaw Festival's first commissioned new play and also won the Voaden Prize. Michael's plays have been produced across Canada and in London, England.

He currently lives in Toronto. In addition to his stage work, his work as a screenwriter includes two produced features and more than 40 television episodes. Projects range from Supervising Story Editor of the "Anne of Green Gables" series to Producer of Queer as Folk.